W9-AQL-169

Barriers to Riches

The Walras-Pareto Lectures, at the École des Hautes Études Commerciales, Université de Lausanne

Barriers to Riches

Stephen L. Parente and
Edward C. Prescott

The MIT Press
Cambridge, Massachusetts
London, England

150109

© 2000 Massachusetts Institute of Technology

All rights reserved. No part of this book may be reproduced in any form by any electronic or mechanical means (including photocopying, record-ing, or information storage and retrieval) without permission in writing from the publisher.

This book was set in Palatino by Asco Typesetters, Hong Kong.

Printed and bound in the United States of America.

Library of Congress Cataloging-in-Publication Data

Parente, Stephen L.
  Barriers to riches / Stephen L. Parente and Edward C. Prescott.
    p.   cm. — (Third Walras-Pareto lecture, University of Lausanne)
  Includes bibliographical references and index.
  ISBN 0-262-16193-1 (alk. paper)
1. Economic development. I. Prescott, Edward C. II. Walras-Pareto
lectures; 3.
HD75.P375   2000
338.9—dc21   00-025414

To Essy and Jan, Our Riches

Contents

Tables

Figures

Preface

This monograph represents the evolution of our thinking on the problem of economic development. Over the course of its chapters we develop a clear and simple theory through a combination of stylized facts, case studies, and quantitative theoretical models drawn from our work in this field over the last decade (Parente and Prescott 1993, 1994, 1999, and Prescott 1998).

Each of us began our inquiry into the problem of development by putting forth models in which savings rates determined growth rates. When we started to examine the data in a systematic way (Parente and Prescott 1993), we were forced to abandon this conceptual framework. We came to the conclusion that relative income levels rather than growth rates are the key to understanding the problem of development.

We next set out to put forth a theory that is consistent with the development facts we documented. The facts themselves dictated certain key features of the theory. Very broadly, the facts suggested a theory of relative incomes. The facts also dictated that the theory must allow for growth in the stock of useable knowledge that is available to all countries. The theory (Parente and Prescott 1994) attempted to explain why all countries do not make

equally efficient use of this knowledge. The theory focused
on firms' decisions to adopt better technologies. It empha-
sized barriers—namely, policy distortions—that affect the
amount of investment a firm has to make to use more of
the stock of useable knowledge in production. We demon-
strated that such a model is consistent with the U.S.
growth facts and the key development facts.

Subsequently, we realized that our theory at the aggregate level is isomorphic to a two-capital stock version of
the neoclassical growth theory with cross-country differences in total factor productivity (TFP). TFP at the aggregate level in a country is a function of the barriers that
constrain the technology choice of firms located there.
What we had in effect shown was that the neoclassical
growth model augmented with intangible capital and with
differences in TFP accounts for the pattern of development. Some—in particular Mankiw et al. (1992) and
Young (1995)—have claimed that the neoclassical growth
model augmented with a second form of capital and with
no differences in TFP accounts for this pattern. We therefore explored quantitatively the validity of this claim (Prescott 1998). From a quantitative theory approach, we found
that this claim is not borne out.

We then proceeded to examine the evidence of differences in barriers and differences in TFP across countries.
We found a large amount of evidence that such differences
exist and that they are important for understanding international income differences. We found that although countries have access to the same stock of knowledge, they
do not all make equally efficient use of this knowledge
because policies in some countries lead to barriers that
effectively prevent firms from adopting more productive
technologies and from changing to more efficient work
practices.

We concluded from this examination that these barriers exist in a large number of instances to protect the vested interests of specialized suppliers of inputs to a particular production process. This insight is important, because our model of technology adoption failed to provide an explanation for why barriers exist and why they differ across countries. We proceeded to formally incorporate this insight into a model of development (Parente and Prescott 1999) and to show how the granting and protection of monopoly rights of industry insiders leads to the inefficient use of inferior technologies. With that paper, we had a theory of differences in TFP. With this theory and our model of technology adoption, we had a theory of economic development and were in a position to write this book.

Acknowledgments

Many individuals have contributed to this effort in one way or another. We have obviously benefited from numerous formal and informal discussions with colleagues in the profession. It is impossible to mention all their names in this space, but a few need to be singled out: Ron Edwards, Alan Heston, Richard Rogerson, Jim Schmitz, and Victor Ríos-Rull all provided us with useful information and insights. We have also benefited from some outstanding research assistance: Jessica Tjornhom, Daria Zakharova, and the support staff at the Federal Reserve Bank of Minneapolis all deserve our thanks. Edward C. Prescott acknowledges financial support from the National Science Foundation. The views expressed herein are those of the authors and not necessarily those of the Federal Reserve Bank of Minneapolis or the Federal Reserve System.

1   Introduction

Differences in living standards across countries are huge. Even after adjusting for differences in relative prices and factoring in household production, the typical person living in a rich country, such as the United States or Switzerland, is twenty to thirty times richer than the typical person living in a poor country, such as Haiti or Nigeria. One of the most important questions facing economists today is: Why do international incomes differ by so much? Or why isn't the whole world as rich as the United States or Switzerland?

We started thinking about this question more than a decade ago, no doubt motivated by the work of Lucas (1988). Over the years, our thoughts have evolved. As in any such process, earlier ideas were refined or were replaced once insights were gained. This question is certainly complex and important enough to warrant another decade or more of thought, but at this stage, the basic tenets of our theory are set. Any changes that are likely to follow will be more in the nature of refinements to our current theme.

Our view is that differences in international incomes are the consequences of differences in the knowledge individual societies apply to the production of goods and services. These differences do not arise because of some fundamental difference in the stock of useable knowledge from which each society can draw. Rather, these differences are the primary result of country-specific policies that result in constraints on work practices and on the application of better production methods at the firm level. Many of these constraints, or barriers, are put in place to protect the interests of groups vested in current production processes. Such barriers at the individual production unit level imply differences in output per unit of the composite input at the aggregate level, that is, differences in total factor productivity (TFP). Most of the differences in international incomes thus are the result of differences in TFP.

The fraction of output a society invests also affects its output per worker by affecting its per worker capital stocks. This fraction is determined by a number of factors such as the nature of its tax system. Differences in the fraction of output countries invest, however, do not contribute significantly to international income differences. There is no systematic relation between savings rates and income levels. The richest industrial country in the world, the United States, has a very low savings rate, much lower in fact than the average for the developing countries. Even the rich, thrifty Swiss have an investment rate significantly below the average of the developing countries.

We are not the first to emphasize the importance of barriers in impeding economic development. Several historians, particularly Rosenberg and Birdzell (1986) and Mokyr (1990), have argued that lower barriers to the adoption and efficient use of technologies are crucial for understanding why modern economic growth—that is, sustained growth in per capita income—began earlier in the West than in the East and began earliest in England. Our work differs from theirs in two important respects. First, in our work dates and locations give way to theory, the quantitative implications of which are derived using general equilibrium methods. Second, our primary concern is with the relative economic performances of countries subsequent to the industrial revolution. More specifically, we are interested in determining whether theory can quantitatively account for the large current differences in international income levels and other key features of the pattern of development.

Our theory distinguishes itself from the literature in several other important ways. First, our theory is one of relative income levels, rather than relative growth rates. Our theory predicts that the growth rate of a country along that country's constant growth path is independent of the size of that country's relative TFP. Our earliest attempts at understanding the problem of development (Prescott and Boyd 1987 and Parente 1994) are not in this category, but instead belong to the endogenous growth literature. Once we examined the empirical evidence, however, we came to the conclusion that we needed to abandon this type of theory. Endogenous growth theory may well prove useful for understanding growth in the stock of knowledge, but it is not useful for understanding international income differences.

This is not to say that growth in the stock of productive knowledge is unimportant in our theory of economic development. It is, in fact, quite important. It is crucial for understanding why western Europe is so much richer today than it was 100 years ago. It is also crucial for understanding how a country like South Korea could increase its per capita output by a factor of six in the twenty-five years starting in 1965—a feat that western European countries never accomplished, not today and not 100 years ago when the average western European was as poor as the average South Korean was in 1965.

The key difference between South Korea in 1965 and western Europe 100 years ago, and between western Europe today and 100 years ago, is the amount of available knowledge that can be applied to the production of goods and services. This stock of useable knowledge has increased dramatically over the last century on account of new discoveries. South Korea in 1965 therefore had a much larger stock of unexploited useable knowledge than western Europe had 100 years ago. South Korea in 1965, however, failed to exploit much of the available stock of productive knowledge because barriers were high there. Western Europe 100 years ago, in contrast, did exploit efficiently the stock of available knowledge and today continues to do so because barriers have been low there.

A necessary precondition for a country to undergo a development miracle is that the country is not exploiting a significant amount of the stock of useable knowledge and therefore is poor relative to the industrial leader. The stock of knowledge will be little exploited if barriers to the adoption and efficient use of this stock are high and have been in place for an extended period. In 1965, many countries besides South Korea met this precondition. Most of these countries today remain poor relative to the leader because unlike South Korea, they did not adopt new policies that greatly reduced barriers to the efficient use of this knowledge. Once South Korea reduced its barriers, thereby greatly increasing its TFP, it experienced a development miracle as it used more of the stock of available knowledge. Western Europe was never in a position to experience a development miracle because it never met the precondition of a large stock of unexploited knowledge.

Although growth in the stock of useable knowledge is important to our theory, we do not attempt to explain here how it increases over time. Our interest is in understanding why some countries are so poor relative to the United States and Switzerland. Poor countries do not need to create new ideas to increase their standard of living. They need only apply existing ideas to the production of goods and services. The relevant question is: Why don't poor countries use the existing stock of useable knowledge more efficiently? This is why the focus of this book is on barriers to the adoption and efficient use of more productive technologies, and not on the creation of more productive technologies.

The adoption of better technologies developed elsewhere may still require some country-specific research and development. In agriculture, for example, research is needed to adapt a technology to specific local requirements. But the frontier research need not take place in each country. As the green revolution in rice and wheat has shown, improved varieties can be developed in international research programs with only modest adaptive research taking place at the local level.

More often than not, the efficient application of ideas developed elsewhere will require investments in both physical and intangible capital. If barriers are absent, these investments will be made. Given people's willingness to forgo current consumption for more future consumption, there will be a period of high investment and rapid convergence to a higher steady-state subsequent to the elimination of some of the barriers to the efficient use of technology. This is precisely what occurred in South Korea and Japan once barriers were reduced.

The fact that some of the necessary capital is not readily available in a country does not in itself pose a barrier to riches. Capital such as equipment or managerial expertise that is not readily available in a country can always be imported from abroad until local supplies can be developed. Rosenberg (1982) and Pack and Nelson (1999) document that Japan and South Korea did just this in going from being relatively poor countries to being relatively rich ones in the postwar period. More recently, the importation of foreign expertise and machines for manufacturing has enabled China to more than double its per capita output in less than ten years.

We begin by documenting some key development facts in chapter 2. We document the degree of income disparity now and in the past and compare the development experiences of different countries and regions. In particular, we compare the development experiences of the East and the West since 1820 and the development experiences of countries correcting for the level of income. The latter set of experiences shows that countries reaching a given per capita income level later in history have been able to double their living standards in fewer years than countries reaching this given level earlier.

We begin with this chapter for two reasons. First, data serve as a test of theory. Second, data can assist in the development of a successful theory. The experience of the East relative to the West since 1950 and the experience of countries that started modern economic growth later are in fact what led us to the conclusion that a theory of relative income levels is more appropriate for understanding the pattern of development than a theory of relative growth rates.

Chapter 3 evaluates neoclassical growth theory as a theory of international income differences. This theory assumes a production technology with constant returns to scale. At a point in time, this technology is common across countries and is characterized by a single aggregate production function with no differences in TFP across countries. With this theory, differences in saving rates give rise to differences in steady-state relative levels of income. In comparison to the data, however, these differences in steady-state relative income levels induced by differences in saving rates are small.

Solow (1957) recognized that growth theory was not a theory of international income levels. Nevertheless, there are several reasons to start with this theory. First, it is consistent with a set of growth facts that hold over time and across countries. Second, the nature of the failure points to how the theory needs to be extended. Third, subsequent to Solow's (1957) formulation, the concept of capital has been broadened to include intangible capital, in particular, human capital. This broadening increases the importance of capital in production, and the greater the importance of capital, the larger the difference in steady-state incomes associated with any given difference in savings rates. The conclusion of our analysis is that even with a broad concept of capital, growth theory still fails as a theory of international income differences as long as TFP is the same across countries. It fails because for differences in savings rates to account for the great disparity in per capita incomes, either intangible capital investment relative to income must be implausibly large, or the returns to such investment must be implausibly large.

Chapter 4 continues to explore the implications of a broader concept of capital for international income differences. A model economy with an educational sector as well as a goods and services production sector is considered. Small differences in time allocated to enhancing human capital can give rise to large differences in steady-state per capita incomes in the model, but only if diminishing

returns to individuals investing in their schooling capital
are small. The problem with this theory is that the implied
time allocated to schooling is implausibly high. Some
direct evidence of the importance of schooling capital differences for international income differences is also reviewed.
We conclude from the analysis and from direct evidence
that adding an education sector to the neoclassical growth
model does not make this model a theory of international
income differences.

These failures lead us to permit TFP to differ across
countries. Chapter 5 evaluates the neoclassical growth
model augmented with intangible capital and with differences in TFP. Evaluation of the model is based on two
particular tests. The first test is whether TFP differences
have to be implausibly large to account for international
income differences. The second test is whether the model
is simultaneously consistent with the Japanese growth
miracle and with investment in intangible capital relative
to GDP being in the reasonable range. We find that the
model passes both tests. The factor difference in TFP
needed to account for the difference in income between the
world's richest and poorest nations is between 2 and 3.
The neoclassical growth model augmented with intangible capital and with differences in TFP accounts remark-
ably well for the huge observed disparity in international
incomes and the rapid development experienced by Japan.

These findings lead us to examine the theory underlying
the aggregate production function of chapter 5. More precisely, we seek to determine what factor or set of factors
give rise at the aggregate level to differences in TFP. Such
differences cannot be the result of cross-country differences in the technology that individual production units
can access. We adhere to the principle, without which
there would be no discipline to the analysis, that model

economies share a common technology. We demonstrate in chapter 6 how policy-induced constraints or barriers at the plant level give rise to differences in TFP at the aggregate level. We consider a barrier that adds to the amount of resources a plant needs to spend in order to access more of the stock of useable knowledge in the world. This barrier is motivated by DeSoto's (1989) study of the effects of excessive regulation and bureaucracy on the level of economic activity in Peru. We aggregate over plants and show that the equilibrium behavior of the economy is identical to that of the neoclassical growth model but with differences in TFP across countries at a point in time. At the chapter's end, we discuss other types of constraints at the plant level and how they, too, map into differences in TFP at the aggregate level. Finally, we show that differences in barriers needed to generate income disparities of the magnitude observed are modest.

We then turn to the data to determine which constraints are more important for understanding differences in productivity. Chapter 7 examines industry data to determine the nature of constraints at the plant level and how policy gives rise to these constraints. The motivation for examining data at the industry level is twofold. First, if differences in policy give rise to differences in TFP at the aggregate level, then policy differences almost surely give rise to differences in TFP at the industry level. Second, industry data have the advantage that the reasons for TFP differences are sometimes transparent. In such cases, there is information as to the nature of the machines used in production and the skills needed to operate this equipment.

The examination of this data leads us to conclude that the most important constraints are on work practices and the use of more productive technologies. Moreover, the examination leads us to hypothesize that whether or not these constraints exist depends upon whether government permits a group to be the sole supplier of an input to the current production process and whether the government protects this monopoly right. In the next chapter, we test this hypothesis.

In chapter 8, we construct a general equilibrium model to assess the quantitative implications of permitting and protecting the right of a group to be the sole supplier of a specialized input to a particular production process. Specifically, we examine whether protected monopoly rights of insiders to various industries can give rise to differences in TFP large enough to account for the disparity in international incomes. Constructing such a model necessarily entails introducing game theoretical elements, because the nature of interaction between groups of factor suppliers with protected monopoly rights and groups that may try to enter an industry with a more efficient production method is strategic. Constructing such a model also entails introducing an agricultural or traditional sector to the economy. The finding of our analysis is that the model restricted to be consistent with observed structural differences between rich and poor countries generates differences in TFP large enough to account for the huge differences in incomes across countries.

Chapter 9 briefly concludes this volume. The chapter summarizes our theory, returns to a number of questions we posed in earlier chapters, and answers them in the context of our theory. Chapter 9 also discusses what types of policies are likely to lead to increases in living standards in the less developed parts of the world. In particular, it discusses the need for free trade and competition to reduce barriers to the adoption and efficient use of knowledge in production.

International Income Facts

Today, huge differences in living standards exist across countries. The richest countries are about thirty times richer than the poorest ones when incomes are measured with the Summers and Heston (1991) purchasing power parity prices. Figure 2.1 depicts the distribution of per capita output relative to the United States in 1988. The set of countries consists of those with 1973 populations exceeding 1 million and for which data over the 1960–1988 period are available.

The difference in living standards between countries is much larger than within-country income differences by most measures. In 1988 the ratio of the per capita income of the country in the 90th percentile to that of the country in the 10th percentile was 20. Within the United States, the ratio of permanent income of an individual in the 90th percentile to an individual in the 10th percentile was less than 4. By this measure, the between-country differences far exceed the within-country differences. Individual differences within a country do not average out across countries.

Huge differences in living standards are a relatively recent phenomenon. Through all but the most recent recorded history, a more or less common living standard characterized all major civilizations. By this we mean that

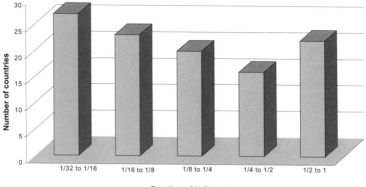

Figure 2.1
Distribution of countries' per capita income relative to U.S. level, 1988
Source: Summers and Heston 1991.

the living standard of the typical person in different societies differed by less than a factor of 2. This living standard was significantly above the subsistence level. In 1688 the poorest quarter of the population in England—the paupers and the cottagers—survived on a consumption level of only one-fourth the national average.[1] Famines did occasionally occur. However, famine was not endemic and almost always was the result of pestilence or war.

The Malthusian model accounts well for this relative constancy of living standards in the period prior to 1800. By the Malthusian model, we mean that population adjusts when output increases so as to maintain the living standard at roughly a common level. Before 1800, there were technological advances that resulted in increases in output per hour. However, these improvements in technology did not lead to large sustained increases in living standards. A rising population facing limited natural resources dissipated most of the gains. This is just what the Malthusian model predicts.

Beginning about 1800, the behavior of international per capita incomes changed. Significant cross-country income differences began to emerge in the first half of the nineteenth century and increased steadily until the middle of the twentieth century. The reason for this increase in income differences across countries is that in some countries incomes began growing rapidly, doubling every thirty-five or forty years, while in other countries incomes remained at the Malthusian level or grew slowly. Sustained rapid increases in per capita output, that is, modern economic growth, started first in England. Shortly thereafter, growth spread to continental Europe and the United States. England was the industrial leader throughout most of the nineteenth century before being surpassed by the United States. Subsequently, the United States has been the industrial leader.

Over the last half of the twentieth century, rapid income growth continued in the leading industrialized countries. International income differences, however, stopped growing, and since 1970, income differences have diminished significantly. There are two reasons why these differences declined. First, virtually all countries experienced modern economic growth, and none stagnated at or near the Malthusian level. Second, on average, countries at all income levels grew as fast as or faster than the industrial leader. Some countries, namely, those that experienced a growth miracle, achieved rates of growth that far exceeded those of the industrial leaders. We now document these facts.

Evolution of Income Levels and Differences

The East and West

Bairoch (1993) argues that in 1800 living standards and resources were comparable in Europe, China, and the

Indian subcontinent. Pomeranz (1998) presents evidence that China and western Europe were quite comparable in terms of resources in 1800. There is some evidence suggesting that this may not have been the case in the Middle East at that time, because in that region the fertility of the soil may have been depleted and most of the forest cut. Given the similarity of the East and West in 1800 and the importance of these regions with nearly 80 percent of the world's population, we compare the subsequent development experiences of the East and West.

For purposes of this comparison, the East consists of all the Eastern countries with current populations exceeding 100 million, namely, China, Pakistan, India, Bangladesh, Indonesia, and Japan, as well as Burma, the Philippines, South Korea, Taiwan, and Thailand. Data unavailability precluded the inclusion of other Eastern countries. The West consists of the western European countries and their ethnic offshoots; this includes all European countries except those that were in the Ottoman Empire and those that were part of the Soviet Union. The former are excluded because they are neither Eastern nor Western; the latter are excluded because there were major changes in the systems of accounts of these countries. The included ethnic offshoots of western Europe are Canada, Mexico, and the United States in North America; Argentina, Brazil, and Chile in South America; and Australia and New Zealand.

Per capita income of each region is the sum of the income of the countries the region comprises divided by the sum of these countries' populations. The data are based on Maddison's (1995) estimates of population and real GDP in 1990 Gheary-Khamis dollars. Table 2.1 shows the relative income differences between the West and the East for various years over the 1820–1992 period. The development experiences of the West and the East are very differ-

Table 2.1
The West versus the East: Per capita income (U.S. dollars, 1990 international prices), 1820–1992

Year	West	East	West/East
1820	1,140	540	2.1
1870	1,880	560	3.3
1900	2,870	680	4.2
1913	3,590	740	4.8
1950	5,450	727	7.5
1973	10,930	1,670	6.5
1989	13,980	2,970	4.7
1992	13,790	3,240	4.3

Source: Maddison 1995.

ent, even though both regions had similar resources and living standards in 1800. The West, with about 20 percent of the world's population, experienced modern economic growth first. Most of the East, with about 60 percent of the world's population, failed to experience modern economic growth until the middle of the twentieth century. The East-West differences in living standards increased continually in the 1820–1950 period. Living standards in the West grew rapidly, while they stagnated or grew slowly in the East. The difference in living standards went from a factor of 2 in 1820 to a factor of 7.5 in 1950.

Bairoch (1993) also provides estimates of incomes and population extending back to the eighteenth century. The Maddison estimates differ slightly from the Bairoch estimates, which put China and the Indian subcontinent on an equal footing with western Europe in 1800. As table 2.1 shows, Maddison estimates that western Europe was two times richer than the East in 1820. He estimates that the East-West income difference began to emerge about 1500 and grew slowly to a factor of 2 by 1820. Bairoch's

Table 2.2
Ratio of West to East per capita income, 1960–1995

Year	West/East
1960	7.3
1973	7.3
1989	5.7
1992	5.2
1995	3.7

Source: Summers and Heston 1991.

(1993) view is that this difference did not begin to emerge until 1800. If Bairoch is correct, the increase between 1820 and 1950 is even larger than reported in table 2.1.

While living standards continued to grow rapidly in the West in the last half of the twentieth century, they grew at an even more rapid rate in the East than in the West after 1950. A consequence of this is that after increasing for roughly 150 years, the income gap between the West and the East decreased dramatically over the last 40 years so that the average person living in the West is now only four times richer than the average person living in the East. This decrease is evident in the Penn World Tables (PWT) data as well.[2] Table 2.2 reports the West and the East development experience in the 1960–1995 period using the PWT5.6 augmented with preliminary population and real GDP estimates for the 1993–1995 period provided to us by Alan Heston. The table confirms that the East narrowed the gap in the 1960–1995 period. The narrowing of the gap is particularly rapid in the latter part of the period with the rapid growth in China with its billion plus people. If current trends continue, it will not be long before differences in living standards between the two regions are eliminated.

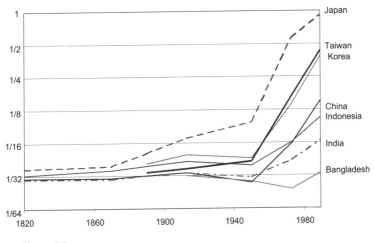

Figure 2.2
Per capita GDP relative to 1985 U.S. level
Source: Maddison 1995.

The beginning of modern economic growth among the countries in the East is far from even, and the rates of increase are far from uniform. Figure 2.2 depicts the time paths of the living standards of a number of these Eastern countries from 1900 to 1985. The data are taken from Maddison (1991). In 1900, all countries' incomes were within a factor of 2, which is not a large difference. With modern growth beginning at different times in different countries and proceeding at different rates, the maximum factor difference in incomes increased to 16 by 1985.

China, which did not enter modern economic growth until 1950, is a particularly interesting country. Chinese development during the 950–1250 period parallels western European development in the 1450–1750 period.[3] Populations and probably living standards roughly doubled, and the rate of innovation increased. Iron production per capita grew by comparable amounts, while the price of iron relative to grain fell by a factor of 4. Commerce and trade increased. Subsequent to these periods of sustained growth, the experiences of China and western Europe diverged. China, while seemingly poised to start modern economic growth once it expelled the Mongolians in the late fourteenth century, failed to do so until 1950. Instead, living standards in China regressed to their tenth century level and remained there for centuries. In Europe, growth accelerated subsequent to 1800, and living standards began doubling every thirty-five or forty years.

The World: 1952–1996

The East in the last half of the twentieth century has been catching up economically with the West. It is not that the West has been progressing at a slower rate than it has since the start of modern economic growth. Rather, it is that the East has grown at a very rapid rate in this period. A question is whether the world, on average, is also catching up with the industrial leader, or is the world continuing to lose ground? To address this question, we abstract from income differences within countries and simply proceed as if all people in a country have the same income level. We then compute the geometric average income relative to the U.S. average level of all people in all countries for which data are available. This is our definition of world mean income level relative to the United States, which was the industrial leader in the years considered.

The calculations are based on Maddison (1995), which reports the data for fifty-six countries. The Maddison set of countries covers all the countries in the world with populations exceeding 20 million, with the exceptions of Algeria, Iran, and Sudan. The total population of included countries is nearly 90 percent of the world's population

Table 2.3
World mean income level relative to the United States, 1952–1996

Year	Percent
1952	13.0
1962	13.3
1972	13.0
1982	13.8
1992	15.1
1996	17.7

Source: Maddison 1995; International Monetary Fund 1998.

in 1992. From this set we deleted the set of seven eastern European countries, which includes the former Soviet Union, because these countries had major changes in their accounting systems, and changes in their income relative to the industrial leader could well be subject to large errors. With this exclusion, our analysis covers 80 percent of the world's population.

The Maddison data cover the 1952–1992 period. Table 2.3 reports estimates for relative world mean income for selected years over the 1952–1996 period. The estimate for 1996 was constructed by using IMF estimates of the growth rate of GDP and population over this period to extend the Maddison data. More specifically, we used the *IMF International Financial Statistics* (1998) to determine real growth in GDP for each country in our data set between 1992 and 1996. We then applied these growth rates to the Maddison 1992 GDP estimates to arrive at 1996 real GDP for each country.

Table 2.3 documents that, on average, there was no catching up in the 1952–1972 period. The western European countries, Japan, South Korea, and Brazil all increased their income significantly relative to the United States in this period. Nevertheless, the world mean income level did not rise relative to the United States. This is because the increase in per capita income in this set of countries was offset by above-average population growth in countries with below-average income. Even if per capita income in a country grows at the same rate as the industrial leader, if that country's per capita income level is below the world mean level and its population growth rate is above average, that country's development experience will lower world mean income relative to the leader. In this period, India, China, Pakistan, Bangladesh, and Indonesia—five countries with half the world's population—were in this category.

Subsequent to 1972, however, world mean income relative to the U.S. level began to increase at an accelerated rate, with the level increasing from 13.0 percent in 1972 to 17.7 percent in 1996. The rapid growth in per capita income in the populous Asian countries and the decline in those countries' population growth rates are responsible for much of this increase. These data clearly show that catching up is occurring in the world in the last quarter of the twentieth century.

Income Mobility

There are two factors behind this catching up documented in table 2.3. First, subsequent to 1960, income in the poorest countries began to rise as fast as the income in the rich, developed countries. No longer did the poorest stagnate as the richest became richer, thereby expanding the gap between the two. For much of the 1960–1995 period, the poorest countries (not including those that experienced protracted armed insurgencies) kept pace with the richest countries. The poorest countries, most of which are in sub-Sahara Africa, are not stuck in a poverty trap. Subsequent to 1960, these countries have been experiencing modern economic growth.

The second factor contributing to this catching up is that a large number of countries out-performed the industrial leader, the United States, which continued to grow at its historical average rate. The dramatic growth subsequent to 1978 in China, with 20 percent of the world's population, played an important role in this catching up. Also playing an important role are the dramatic growth experiences in a number of countries in the 1955–1990 period. In the 25-year 1955–1980 period, Japan increased its per capita output by a factor of 5, as did Taiwan in the 1965–1990 period. South Korea had an even more remarkable development experience in the 25-year 1965–1990 period, increasing its per capita product 6.3 times. Such development experiences are miracles.

All of these growth miracles are a recent phenomenon and are limited to countries that initially were far behind the industrial leader when their miracle began. No country at the top of the income distribution has increased its per capita income by a factor of 4 in twenty-five years. It has always taken the leaders at least eighty years to increase per capita income by a factor of 4. This suggests that the potential for rapid growth is greater the farther behind a country is from the industrial leader. Late entrants to modern economic growth have, in fact, typically doubled their per capita incomes in far less time than early entrants did. For instance, Taiwan in 1965 had the same living standard that the United States achieved in 1855. Taiwan took a mere ten years to double that standard of living. The United States, in contrast, took forty-four years to accomplish this same feat.

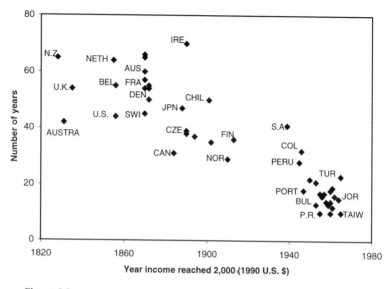

Figure 2.3
Years for per capita income to grow from 2,000 to 4,000 (1990 U.S. $)
Source: See the appendix.

Figure 2.3 documents this general pattern. It plots the number of years a country took to go from 10 percent to 20 percent of the 1985 U.S. per capita income level versus the first year that country achieved the 10 percent level. The 1985 U.S. level was 20,000 in 1990 dollars. The set of countries considered had at least 1 million people in 1970 and had achieved and sustained a per capita income of at least 10 percent of the 1985 U.S. level by 1965. There are fifty-six countries that fit these criteria and for which data are available. Of these fifty-six countries, all but four managed to double their per capita income by 1992. The four exceptions all had protracted armed insurgencies that disrupted their development.[4] The construction of figure 2.3 is described in detail in the appendix.

The difference in the length of the doubling period between the sets of late and early entrants to modern economic growth is dramatic. For early entrants, which are
defined as those achieving 10 percent of the 1985 U.S. level
before 1950, the median length of the doubling period is
45 years. For late entrants, which are defined as those
achieving 10 percent of the 1985 U.S. level after 1950, the
median length of the doubling period is 15 years.

The choice of starting level is not important. A similar
pattern emerges when the starting level is fixed at 5 percent and at 20 percent of the 1985 U.S. level. For those
countries achieving 20 percent of the 1985 U.S. level prior
to 1950, the median doubling period is 37 years. For those
countries achieving this level after 1950, the median doubling period is 14 years.[5] For a starting level of 5 percent
of the 1985 U.S. level, the median period is 60 years for
those countries that achieved and sustained that level
prior to 1950.[6] For countries that achieved and sustained
that level after 1950, the median doubling period is 26.5
years. Late entrants into modern economic growth typically double their per capita income in far less time than
early entrants did.

Summary of Facts

A summary of our findings is as follows:

1. Subsequent to 1800, per capita income of the leading
industrial country grew at a rapid rate, doubling every
forty years.

2. Prior to 1800, living standards differed little across
countries and across time.

3. Differences in living standards increased dramatically
between 1800 and 1950 as the West grew rich and the rest
of the world stagnated or grew slowly.

4. Differences between the West and the East declined after 1950 as most countries in the East started modern economic growth, and most grew even faster than most countries in the West.

5. World differences in living standards have declined over the 1960–1988 period as modern economic growth has been achieved by almost every country in the world and the East has narrowed the West's lead.

6. Growth miracles have occurred, but only in countries that were well behind the leader at the time the miracle began.

7. Countries reaching a given level of income at a later date typically double that level in a shorter time.

Some Questions and Features of Candidate Theory

These facts raise a number of questions. In particular, why did modern economic growth begin at different times and proceed at different rates? Why did it not begin in China in the late fourteenth century after the Mongolian invaders were expelled? Why did modern economic growth start first in England before it started in continental Europe? Why did the United States surge past Britain in the late nineteenth century to become the industrial leader? Why did growth miracles occur in some countries and not in other similar ones? These are important questions that a theory of development must answer. The rest of this volume is devoted to trying to answer these questions.

These facts lead us to search for a theory with certain features. The difference in timing of entry into modern economic growth leads us to search for a theory in which policy determines the timing of entry. Given economic institutions or policies, when knowledge reaches a critical level, modern economic growth begins. Growth miracles lead us to search for a theory in which changes in policy can result in a period of rapid convergence to a higher income level relative to the industrial leader. The failure of any industrial leader to experience a growth miracle leads us to search for a theory for which this is not possible; that is, the level of the idustrial leader primarily grows because of the accumulation of useable knowledge. Finally, the narrowing of the gap between the industrial leader and the rest of the world that has occurred subsequent to 1970 also leads us to search for a theory of relative income differences. The reason is that increases in interactions among people throughout the world should result in more countries' adopting the better economic institutions of the rich industrialized nations. Thus we are led to consider theories of relative income differences whereby a country's policy determines when it enters modern economic growth and, once having done so, determines its income relative to the leader. We now turn to the neoclassical growth model, a theory of relative income levels.

Appendix: Large Rapid Development Experiences

This appendix describes the construction of figure 2.3. The countries we consider are the non–oil-producing countries with 1970 populations of 1 million or more that had attained 10 percent of the 1985 U.S. per capita output level by 1965. The figure plots on the horizontal axis the first year in which such a country attained 10 percent of the 1985 U.S. per capita output level against the number of years for the country to achieve 20 percent of that level.

The sources of the data used to construct the figure are Maddison (1995) and the Summers and Heston (1991) Penn World Table 5.6 (PWT5.6). Maddison provides estimates of GDP per capita and population for fifty-six countries over the 1820–1992 period. Data going back to 1820 are not available for all countries. Before 1890, if data are available, they are for only three years: 1820, 1850, and 1870. After 1890, data are available on a yearly basis for many, but not all, countries in the study. Outputs are valued in 1990 U.S. dollars. In contrast to his past estimates, Maddison (1995) uses Gheary-Khamis international prices rather than U.S. prices to value each country's quantities of final goods and services. The quantities in all years are valued in 1990 international prices.

For those countries not covered by Maddison (1995, table 1.3) and that have attained 10 percent of 1985 U.S. per capita output after 1950, we use the PWT5.6, which provides yearly data for the 1950–1992 period for 152 countries. Observations for some countries in some years are not available. The Gheary-Khamis procedure to determine international prices is similarly employed. In contrast to Maddison (1995), Summers and Heston (1991) provide estimates of GDP both in 1985 international prices and in year t international prices.

Summers and Heston (1991) provide two measures of labor productivity in addition to GDP per capita. These other two measures are GDP per equivalent adult and GDP per worker. The number of equivalent adults equals the population over the age of fifteen plus one-half of the population under the age of fifteen. The number of workers is determined using estimates of labor force participation rates from the International Labor Organization.

For the postwar period analysis, we use a measure that is based on equivalent adults rather than on total population. In trying to understand why an individual in the United States produces more than a worker in India, the per equivalent adult output measure is more informative than the per capita measure. The per worker output is even more informative. However, we do not use that measure because we have greater confidence in the accuracy of the equivalent adult estimates.

Our per equivalent adult measure differs slightly from the real GDP per equivalent adult measure in the PWT5.6, denoted *RGDPEA*. Our measure is constructed from the date t GDP of countries relative to the date t U.S. GDP in date t international prices provided in the PWT5.6. To these date t relative outputs, we multiply the ratio of year t GDP to 1985 U.S. GDP that use a chain index and international prices. These relative levels for the United States for different dates with a chain index and international prices correspond to the *RGDPEA* numbers for the United States in the PWT5.6.

Effectively, in our procedure, the United States acts as a link between two points in time, thus allowing the comparison of a country's GDP across those two dates. Some measure of world GDP that used international prices and chain indexes to connect these points in time would have been better to use. However, such a measure is not available. The United States is the next best alternative for making this connection across two points in time, because its data are reliable. The United States has been the leading industrialized country, as measured by output per capita, since 1890, and it produces a diverse basket of goods. That diversity is important because the effect of a change in relative prices on U.S. output is likely to be small compared to the effect of such a change on the output of a country specializing in only a handful of goods.

An alternative procedure for comparing a country's output across two points in time, and the one that underlies the Summers and Heston (1991) numbers, is to pick a year and a unit of account and get a country's relative

GDP for that year in those year prices and that unit of account. In Summers and Heston, the year is 1990 and the unit of account is U.S. dollars. When a chain index is applied to this number, the relative GDP at different dates for the country is then determined. A nice feature of our procedure over the alternative one used by Summers and Heston is that the relative GDP of countries at a point in time is independent of which year-country unit of account is used. For the alternative procedure, the relative GDP of countries in a given year may differ if a different year-country unit of account is used. Effectively, a country's GDP relative to another's can change from one year to the next simply because relative prices change. This alternative procedure cannot capture the effect of relative price changes on relative wealths.

The PWT5.6 does not actually report year t GDP per equivalent adult in year t international prices, which are used in the first stage of our procedure to construct our output measures. However, these year t GDP per equivalent adult numbers in year t international prices can be easily calculated from the tables in three steps: In the first step, use year t GDP per capita of country i together with year t GDP per equivalent adult that use international prices and chain indices ($RCDPCH$ and $RGDPEA$, respectively, in the PWT5.6) to determine the ratio of the population to equivalent adults for country i in year t. Denote this ratio by $(n_{i,t}/a_{i,t})$. In the second step, convert each country's date t GDP per capita in year t prices provided in the PWT5.6 (CGDP) to a per equivalent adult measure by multiplying it by this ratio $(n_{i,t}/a_{i,t})$. In the last step, divide this year t per equivalent adult GDP number in year t prices for country i by the date t U.S. GDP per equivalent adult number in date t prices. Denote this resulting number by $x_{i,t}$. The relative output levels for the

United States, chained and in international prices, that are
used in the second stage of our procedure come directly
from the PWT5.6. They correspond to the variable denoted
by *RGDPEA* in those tables. Formally, our measure of
relative output is equal to

$$x_{i,t} \cdot \frac{RGDPEA_{us,t}}{RGDPEA_{us,85}}.$$

According to the PWT5.6 and the *World Development
Report 1994*, there were 124 countries in 1970 with populations of 1 million or more. Four of these countries, Saudi
Arabia, Kuwait, Libya, and Venezuela, were oil-producing
nations and thus have been removed from our population
of countries. Of the set of 120 non–oil-producing countries
with 1970 populations in excess of 1 million, fifty-six had
attained 10 percent of U.S. 1985 real GDP per capita by
1965 according to the PWT5.6. Another fifty-six, according
to the PWT5.6, had not. The other eight countries that
make up the total are not covered in the PWT5.6. Of these
eight countries, the *World Development Report 1994* clearly
shows that five had not attained 10 percent of the 1985
U.S. level by 1965. These five countries are Afghanistan,
Albania, Cambodia, Vietnam, and Yemen, P.D.R. For the
other three countries not covered in the PWT5.6, the data
that are available are inconclusive as to whether these
countries had reached the 10 percent level by 1965. These
countries are Cuba, Lebanon, and North Korea.

Of the fifty-six countries that had attained 10 percent of
1985 U.S. per capita output by 1965, only four had not
attained 20 percent of this level by 1990. These countries
are Guatemala, El Salvador, Nicaragua, and Papua New
Guinea. All four countries had long, protracted armed
insurgencies that disrupted development. Additionally,
Papua New Guinea was not an independent country until

1975. This leaves the number of countries actually plotted at fifty-two.

Table A.1 lists the names of these fifty-two countries as well as the estimated year at which each attained 10 percent of the 1985 U.S. per capita output and the number of years it took each to reach 20 percent of that level. Countries for which the data are taken from the PWT5.6 are indicated with an asterisk. All others are from Maddison (1995). The PWT5.6 data are used for only those countries not covered by Maddison in his 1820–1992 study.

Several countries, not covered by Maddison, have productivity slightly above 10 percent of the 1985 U.S. level the first year they appear in the PWT5.6. For these countries, we took the period that each took to double from its level in the first year it appears in the PWT5.6. These countries and their real output in the first year they appear in the PWT5.6 are Namibia (0.12), Puerto Rico (0.14), Hong Kong (0.14), Iran (0.13), Iraq (0.12), and Israel (0.12).

Only two countries, not covered by Maddison, had a productivity well above the 10 percent level the first year they appeared in the PWT5.6. These two countries are East Germany and Uruguay. To determine the doubling period for East Germany, we assumed that it had the same level of per capita output in all years preceding its formation as West Germany had. To determine the doubling period for Uruguay, we assumed that it had the same per capita output as Argentina in all years prior to becoming a moderate income country. The relevant data for Argentina and West Germany are taken from Maddison.

For the countries covered by Maddison, we encountered two data-related problems that necessitated particular adjustments. The first problem relates to the fact that yearly data for most countries are not given until 1890. Prior to this date, data for these countries are given at

Table A.1
Number of years to develop from low- to middle-income economy

Country	Starting date	Number of years
New Zealand	1821	65
Australia	1831	42
United Kingdom	1835	54
Netherlands	1855	64
Belgium	1856	55
United States	1856	44
Hungary	1870	65
Italy	1870	54
Spain	1870	57
Austria	1870	60
Switzerland	1870	45
USSR	1870	66
France	1872	54
West Germany	1872	55
East Germany	1872	55
Denmark	1872	50
Canada	1884	31
Sweden	1888	47
Ireland	1890	70
Czechoslovakia	1890	39
Argentina	1890	38
Uruguay	1890	38
Japan	1894	37
Chile	1901	50
Greece	1902	35
Norway	1910	29
Finland	1913	36
South Africa	1939	41
Peru	1945	28
Colombia	1946	32
Portugal	1947	18
Mexico	1950	22
Poland	1950	22

Table A.1 (continued)

Country	Starting date	Number of years
Iraq*	1953	21
Bulgaria	1953	13
Iran*	1955	17
Puerto Rico*	1955	10
Jamaica*	1956	16
Brazil	1957	17
Yugoslavia	1958	14
Panama*	1959	13
Romania	1962	16
Ecuador*	1960	18
Malaysia*	1960	18
Namibia*	1960	14
Hong Kong*	1960	10
Singapore*	1960	10
Costa Rica*	1961	19
Syria*	1961	12
Jordan*	1964	15
Taiwan	1965	10
Turkey	1965	23

Source: Maddison 1995; *Summers and Heston 1991.

most for years 1820, 1850, and 1870. Several countries, clearly, had achieved 10 percent of the 1985 U.S. level in a year between these data points. For these countries, we interpolated geometrically to determine the first year each had attained 10 percent of the 1985 U.S. level. New Zealand had attained 10 percent of the 1985 U.S. productivity before the first year in which data are given. To determine New Zealand's starting year, we geometrically extrapolated backward.

The second problem relates to the disruptions in output associated with World War II. For those countries that began with 10 percent before the war, and for which the war was a major disruption in economic activity, we used the doubling period going back from the level of productivity each country attained prior to the war's beginning. The countries and the adjustments that were made are as follows: we use the period that Austria went from 0.09 to 0.18, Czechoslovakia went from 0.075 to 0.15, the U.S.S.R. went from 0.05 to 0.10, Hungary went from 0.06 to 0.12, Italy went from 0.07 to 0.14, Spain went from 0.07 to 0.14, Japan went from 0.05 to 0.10 percent, and Greece went from 0.065 to 0.12. For Greece, we extrapolated backward to determine this doubling period because data did not go back far enough in time. The only exception to this rule is Poland. Because of the lack of data in the years leading up to World War II, we had no choice for Poland but to use the doubling period starting with the first year after the war that is given. The period corresponds to the number of years Poland took to go from 0.12 to 0.24.

Lastly, we note that two countries, South Korea and Thailand, by 1990 achieved 20 percent of the 1985 U.S. productivity, but are not included in table A1 because they did not attain 10 percent until after 1965. South Korea, according to Maddison, accomplished this feat in eight years beginning in 1969. Thailand, according to Maddison, did it in thirteen years starting in 1977.

3   Growth Theory with No TFP Differences

We begin with the question of whether neoclassical growth theory can account for the large international differences in incomes and the patterns of development documented in chapter 2. The neoclassical production function is the cornerstone of the theory and is used in virtually all applied aggregate analyses. The aggregate production function is used in public finance exercises to evaluate the consequences of alternative tax policies. (See, for example, Auerbach and Kotlikoff 1987 and Chari et al. 1994.) Jorgenson and Yun (1984), Shoven and Whalley (1984), and many others use multisector generalizations to address policy issues.

An appealing feature of this simple construct is that it accounts for the balanced growth that has characterized the U.S. economy for nearly two centuries; also it deals with well-defined aggregate inputs and outputs. A final appealing feature is that it is based upon a lot of theory. The aggregate production function specifies maximum output given the quantities of the inputs. If the plant size needed to realize all the economies of scale is small relative to total output and if entry and exit is permitted, profit maximization and competitive factor markets result in output being maximized given the aggregate factor inputs. Thus this theory is a theory of the income side of national income and product accounts (NIPA) as well as a theory of production.

For the standard growth model to be a theory of the international relative income differences, the size of per worker capital stocks across countries must account for differences in output per hour worked, because with this theory, total factor productivity (TFP) is common across countries. According to the model, rich countries are rich because they have accumulated large per worker stocks of capital. Differences in stocks of capital are the result of differences in past savings rates. If savings rates are constant over time, the country with a higher savings rate will have a higher per worker output.

The Standard Model

In evaluating the neoclassical growth model as a theory of international income differences, we restrict the model to be consistent with a set of growth facts that hold over time and across countries. These facts deal with ratios of nominal quantities, so there are no index number problems. One fact is the constancy of factor income shares over time and across countries. In estimating labor share, we assign wage and salary income to labor. We use Kravis's (1959) economywide assumption to assign a fraction of indirect business taxes and proprietors' income to labor. With this economywide assumption, the share of these components that are labor income is assumed to be the same as for the economy as a whole. The labor income share in the United States has fluctuated around the 70 percent level, while the real wage has increased steadily. The time series evidence is that the labor share varies little with the level of income.

Gollin (1997) presents cross-sectional evidence that the labor share and the level of development are unrelated as well. He finds, using the same income assignment rules we used, that labor shares are concentrated at about 70 percent across countries with no relation to the level of development. An implication of this fact is that the real wage is roughly proportional to per worker output.

Another fact is that the average return on tangible assets for rich and poor countries is about 5 percent. The average return on capital is estimated as follows. An estimate of total return on capital and land is obtained by summing corporate profits, rental income, net interest income, 30 percent of proprietors' income, and 30 percent of indirect business taxes. This sum is then divided by the value of private capital and land to obtain the average return.

These facts dictate the choice of a Cobb-Douglas production function with its unit elasticity of substitution between capital and labor services. If the elasticity were not unity, factor share would be related to per worker output. When the Cobb-Douglas production function is used, the growth model specifies per worker output y as a function of per worker capital k as follows:

$$y_t = A(1 + \gamma)^{(1-\theta)t} k_t^{\theta},$$

where $0 < \theta < 1$ is the capital share parameter and $(1 + \gamma)^{1-\theta} - 1 > 0$ is the rate of growth of TFP. The resource constraint for this economy is $c_t + x_t \le y_t$, where c is per worker consumption and x is per worker gross capital formation. The law of motion of the per worker capital stock is

$$k_{t+1} = (1 - \delta)k_t + x_t,$$

where $0 < \delta < 1$ is the depreciation rate.

Savings Rates and Steady-State Relative Income

In this model, savings rates have no effect on growth rates along the constant growth path. Per capita variables in all countries grow at the common rate γ. Savings rates do affect relative steady-state income levels. Savings rates may vary across countries for a number of policy-related reasons, such as the nature of the tax system. A question, then, is whether differences in gross savings rates across countries can account for a significant part of the difference in levels of development. If the answer to this question is no, there is no need to proceed to the question of why savings rates differ. Consequently, we begin our evaluation of the growth theory by assuming a given gross savings rate.

If the gross savings rate is s, so that $x_t = s y_t$, (per worker) output will converge to

$$y_t = A(1 + \gamma)^t [As/(\delta + \gamma)]^{\theta/(1-\theta)}.$$

It follows from the above equation that the effect of different savings rates for relative steady-state incomes depends only on the value of the capital share parameter, θ. A value of 0.25 for this parameter is consistent with U.S. growth observations, as labor's share is roughly 70 percent and a reasonable value for land share is 5 percent. The values of the other parameters in the above equation, including the value of TFP, are not relevant in the context of this exercise because they are assumed not to differ across model economies.

For a capital share restricted to match U.S. growth observations, savings rates have small effects upon steady-state income levels. This is shown in table 3.1, which reports relative steady-state levels of output as a function of the savings rates. Changing the savings rate by a fac-

Table 3.1
Steady-state effects of savings rates on income levels

Savings rate	Relative income level (%)
.10	.79
.20	1.00
.30	1.15
.40	1.26

Table 3.2
Fraction of GDP invested, 1966–1993

	Industrialized countries	Developing countries	Africa
1966	22.7	17.6	19.0
1970	23.7	17.5	22.9
1975	21.6	25.5	29.2
1980	23.2	25.5	28.0
1985	21.3	22.3	20.3
1990	21.5	24.3	19.6
1993	19.4	23.3	18.8

Source: International Monetary Fund 1994.

tor of 2 changes steady-state relative income only by a factor of 1.25, and not a factor of 20. Savings rates in the rich countries would have to be 8,000 times higher than in the poor countries to account for a factor 20 difference in output levels.

The empirical evidence does not even support the proposition that rich countries save a higher fraction of their output. Table 3.2 reports investment as a percentage of GDP averaged for the set of industrialized countries and for the set of developing countries for various years over the 1966–1993 period. These averages are from the International Monetary Fund (1994). Over this period, the frac-

tions of output that rich and poor countries invest
have been roughly the same. Since 1975, the fraction of
product invested has been slightly higher for the developing countries than for the industrialized countries. The absence of any significant difference in savings rates between
the rich and poor countries over this period is not being
driven by the high savings rates in Singapore, South Korea,
and Taiwan, either. We also report in table 3.2 the fraction
of output invested for Africa over the 1966–1993 period,
which is not much different from the fraction of output
invested in the set of rich countries over this period. Differences in the fraction of output invested do not account
for differences in international per capita incomes.

Mismeasured Capital

With this model and common TFP across countries, absent
tax and other distortions, the price of investment goods
relative to consumption goods should be constant across
countries. Easterly (1993), Jones (1994), and Restuccia and
Urrutia (1996), using various versions of the Summers and
Heston PWTs, find that the prices of investment goods
in terms of consumption goods are substantially higher in
poor countries. When the fraction of product invested
in each country is adjusted for these differences in relative prices, as they are in the Summers and Heston (1991)
purchasing power parity (PPP) approach, investment to
output ratios vary systematically with the level of development. This has led some to conclude that capital-output
ratios are smaller in the poor countries and that these differences can account for a significant part of international
income differences.[7]
  Defining the stock of capital is conceptually problem-
atic, and measuring the defined concept is difficult in

practice. The capital stock estimates in the PWTs incorporate these relative price differences across countries. The Summers and Heston (1991) procedure is as follows. They use price data collected in the United Nations International Price Comparison Programme benchmark studies. In a benchmark study, price data are sought for about 1,500 commodities of which approximately a quarter are investment goods. Investment goods are broken down into five categories. For rich countries, the actual number of prices collected in a study is about 1,110, and for poor countries, from 400 to 700. The Summers (1973) method is used to construct a PPP index for each category of goods. With this method, if all prices are available, the index is the geometric average of the prices. The price index for investment goods is divided into the expenditures on these goods to arrive at a real investment number. To construct capital stocks, U.S. useful lives and the perpetual inventory method are used for each of five broad categories of investment goods. The aggregate capital stock is the sum of these five stocks.

There are a number of potential problems with this procedure. Useful lives are probably longer in poor countries given that the price of maintenance is low in those countries (Heston and Summers 1996). In addition, with exchange rates, the reason the price of investment goods relative to consumption goods is so much higher in poor countries is that consumption goods are cheap in poor countries and not that investment goods are expensive. If one takes the price indices of investment goods in the PWTs and converts them into a single currency using exchange rates, one finds that investment goods cost about 30 percent more in the poorest countries than they do in the richest countries. If one does the same for the price indices of consumption goods, one finds that consumption goods cost two or three times more in the richest countries than they do in the poorest countries. This suggests that nontradable consumption goods and services are important in explaining why the relative prices of investment goods are so much higher in poor countries.

Even when the PWT numbers are taken as adequate measures of the capital service inputs and the outputs, and they are the best available, differences in investment-output ratios account for little of the difference in per worker output. To see this, we first compute the TFP for each country implied by the PWT per worker output and capital stock numbers. Next, we endow each country with a capital stock that gives it the same capital-output ratio as the United States. With these endowments and imputed TFPs, we calculate the implied output for each country. Differences in these imputed outputs, therefore, reflect only differences in TFP. Lastly, we compare the standard deviation of the logarithm of PWT output numbers to the standard deviation of the logarithm of our imputed output numbers.

This exercise uses only countries that had a population exceeding 1 million in 1985 and that have participated in at least one United Nations International Price Comparison Programme benchmark study, that is, countries for which some prices were collected for at least one year. The size of the sample is fifty-seven. The important finding is that the standard deviation of the logarithm of per worker output implied by the imputed TFPs is reduced by only 11 percent. With these calculations, differences in capital that are due to differences in investment share of total product account for 11 percent of the differences, while differences in TFP account for 89 percent. We conclude that even if international rather than domestic prices are used, differences in investment share of product account for little of the differences in per worker output.

The Two-Sector Extension

The relative price of investment goods relative to consumption goods also differs across time within a country. In the United States the relative price of durable goods has fallen over time.[8] With the assumed neoclassical production technology, the prices of the investment good and the consumption good, absent corners, are equal in equilibrium. For the purposes that we use the model and the statistics to which we match the structure, the secular decline in the relative price of durables is not a problem. The model can be extended so that it matches this secular decline by introducing a durable good sector and assuming that technological change is more rapid in this sector than in the consumption good sector. With such a technology, the relative price of capital goods, in which one unit of capital provides one unit of capital services, declines secularly. The conclusion that the neoclassical growth model is not a theory of international income differences still holds with this extension.

The following two-sector model establishes this point. The consumption good sector has the production function

$$c_t = A k_{ct}^{\theta} n_{ct}^{1-\theta}.$$

The investment good sector has the production function

$$x_t = A(1+\gamma)^{(1-\theta)t/\theta} k_{xt}^{\theta} n_{xt}^{1-\theta}.$$

All variables are per worker. The capital share parameter is assumed to be the same for these two sectors because capital and labor shares of value added vary little across highly aggregated industrial sectors. In this world, all the technology change is in the investment good sector, and none is in the consumption good sector. A worker's time endowment, which is normalized to 1, is split between the two sectors so that $1 = n_{ct} + n_{xt}$. Similarly, the capital stock, k_t, is split between the two sectors so that $k_t = k_{ct} + k_{xt}$. As before, capital depreciates at rate δ, so

$$k_{t+1} = (1 - \delta)k_t + x_t.$$

If the savings rate is constant, that is, the ratio of the value of investment to output in current prices is constant, the economy converges to a growth path in which c grows at the constant rate γ and both x and k grow at the rate $(1 + \gamma)^{1/\theta} - 1$. The price of the investment good relative to the consumption good, q, declines at the rate $(1 + \gamma)^{1-1/\theta} - 1$. In the steady state, the value of investment as a share of output is a constant share of output. Thus, this technology is consistent with the U.S. growth fact that investment share has been more or less constant in current prices, even though the price of investment has declined relative to the price of consumption. In constant prices, of course, investment share of product has increased over the last fifty years.

The effect of savings rates on relative steady-state incomes in this two-sector model is the same as in the one-sector standard model. It is straightforward to show that per worker output for an economy with a gross savings rate $s = q_t x_t / y_t$ converges to exactly the same expression as for the one-sector growth model. Consequently, for capital's share restricted to match U.S. growth observations, savings rate differences have tiny consequences for international income differences.

The Intangible Capital Extension

Intangible Capital Investment

From the point of view of theory, investment is any allocation of resources that is designed to increase future production possibilities. NIPA investment equals the value of new structures and equipment plus changes in inventory. NIPA investment systematically understates the proportion of resources devoted to what corresponds to investment in the theory. For instance, maintenance and repair expenditures are undertaken to enhance future products possibilities but yet are not part of NIPA investment because these outlays are expensed in the NIPA. A second category of investment expenditures, nearly all of which are not included in NIPA investment, consists of investments in intangible capital. The omission of these other forms of investments from NIPA is relevant for evaluating neoclassical growth theory as a theory of international income differences. If investment is sufficiently important relative to consumption, arbitrarily small differences in savings rates can give rise to arbitrarily large differences in steady-state per capita incomes. Consequently, a redefinition of income and product that includes maintenance and investments in intangible capital is needed to assess how savings rates affect steady-state incomes.

To redefine income and product, it is first necessary to identify investments in intangible capital. The guiding principle is whether an activity affects future output as opposed to current output. Clearly, the creation of new businesses meets this criteria. Entrepreneurs, in setting up new enterprises, make huge investments in the form of forgone wages. Most of these new enterprises turn out to be unsuccessful. The costs for both the successful and the unsuccessful, including the forgone wages, must be included in the redefinition of investment.

Entrepreneurs are not the only ones making investments in creating new production possibilities. Within established enterprises, large amounts of resources are allocated to developing and launching new products. Large amounts of resources are also allocated in these establishments to increasing the efficiency of existing production processes. The value of all these resources must be included in this extended definition of investment.

Research and development and software also must be included. Most research and development and most software, whether purchased or developed internally, is not capitalized under the current U.S. system of accounts. Software has a long life, typically longer than the computers, which are capitalized and therefore part of measured investment. Indeed, as evidenced by the Y2K problem, this life can be extremely long. Software purchased or developed by the government should also be included in investment.

The value of the resources allocated to increasing the organization capital of firms must also be included. Investments in organizational capital include the value of the time engineers spend developing more efficient production methods, the time managers spend matching people with tasks, the time managers spend learning about current and prospective employees, and the time staff spend learning who within the organization has access to needed information and skills. Investments in organizational capital also include the value of resources allocated to learning about products and services of other firms that are used in production and to making other firms aware of the potential use of the selling firm's products. Some advertising expenditures serve a similar purpose, except they serve to educate consumers. The value of these resources is part of intangible capital investment.

Other resource allocations increase the human capital of individuals rather than a firm's organizational capital, as the capital is embodied in individual workers. Their value must also be included in the extended definition of investment. Businesses allocate a large amount of resources to training their workforce. Workers also learn by themselves through repeating tasks. Individuals acquire human capital outside of firms through schooling. In this case, the investments include the forgone wages of individuals as well as the direct cost of the training program.

The size of these unmeasured investments relative to GDP is a crucial issue for determining the effects of savings rates on relative steady-state income levels. What is the size of these unmeasured investments? The key to answering this question is determining what fraction of economic activity is concerned with future as opposed to current output. There are at least two ways to come up with an estimate of this fraction. The first way follows from the answer to the question: how much could inputs be reduced without reducing measured current output? Eliminating research and development activities, new software purchases and development, personnel offices, the major part of informational technology offices, skill training programs, central headquarters, advertising activities, people searching for better suppliers, and most managers would not lower current output. There have been cases of large reductions in the size of organizations with little decline in output in the short run. Let us assume that inputs can be reduced by one-third without reducing current measured output when the time period is a year.[9] If so, then two-thirds of resources are being used to produce c and x_k and one-third is being used to produce x_z. This assumption implies that unmeasured investment, x_z, is one-half of GDP, $c + x_k$. That is, unmeasured investment is 50 percent of GDP.

A second way to estimate the size of unmeasured investment is to add up estimates of intangible investments. Maintenance and repair, one form of investment in intangible capital, are a large percentage of GDP. In Canada, a typical industrial country, these costs are reported by the *Canadian Minerals Yearbook* (1998) to be over 5 percent of GDP. Research and development, and businesses and governments in the United States total 3 percent of GDP. This number must be tripled in the estimate of unmeasured investment because research and development expenditures do not reflect the costs of perfecting the new manufacturing processes and new products or launching the new products.[10] Investment in software has increased in the 1990s. Its cost is sizeable. Meltzer (1993) estimates that this unmeasured investment in the United States in 1990 is 1 percent of GDP. Given that this investment has been growing at 16 percent a year, it is about 3 percent of GDP in the late 1990s. Together maintenance, research and development, and software are in the neighborhood of 17 percent of GDP.

To this number, we must add firms' investment in organization capital. The size of these investments is surely large. The large and prolonged increases in productivity associated with firm-specific learning-by-doing, such as those documented in the U.S. semiconductor industry by Irwin and Klenow (1994) and in the Swedish iron industry by Lundberg (1961), provide more evidence that sizeable investments are being made. The exact size of these investments is not clear. However, we see 12 percent of GDP as being plausible.

Investment in human capital is the final form of investment not included in NIPA investment numbers. This investment is large, being every bit as large as investment in organization capital. For instance, the value of resources used up in the process of learning how to use software is probably greater than the value of the computer. This learning on the job is an investment from the point of view of theory. The wage-earning experience profile can be used to estimate on-the-job human capital investment. Assuming (1) that total compensation is the sum of human capital gained and the employee compensation included in the NIPA, (2) that total compensation is equal to total marginal product, and (3) that this investment is zero the period before retirement, unmeasured on-the-job investment in human capital is 7.5 percent of GDP.[11] This number is probably too low for two reasons. First, there is probably some smoothing of wage payments over the career of a worker to facilitate consumption smoothing. Second, many skills are firm-specific and are financed by the firm. The returns on these investments would not show up in the experience-earnings profile. Given these two considerations, a plausible estimate of on-the-job investment in training and skill acquisition is 10 percent of GDP.

Since increases in human capital come about through schooling as well as on-the-job learning, the costs of schooling are a human capital investment. Mincer (1994) estimates that schooling costs for the U.S. economy are a little over 10 percent of GDP. This number includes student opportunity costs. This number is an upper bound, because not all expenditures on education are investment in market human capital—some are consumption. Elementary schools provide valued babysitting services. Sports and other extracurricular activities are valued in themselves. Some of schooling investment is in nonmarket human capital. Learning to better appreciate literature and the arts, for example, is an investment in nonmarket human capital. For these reasons, this 10 percent number for schooling investment in market capital is too high. We think a more reasonable number for schooling investment in market human capital is 5 percent of GDP.

Summing these estimates over all forms of unmeasured investment, our estimate of aggregate unmeasured investment is 48 percent of GDP. This is a large number. It is close to the back-of-the-envelope estimate obtained using the first method. It is approximately equal to the number of Chari et al. (1997). We conclude from these exercises that unmeasured investment is big and could be as much as 50 percent of GDP and is surely at least 30 percent of GDP.

The Model Economy Calibrated to U.S. Data

To see if adding intangible capital can make the neoclassical growth model a theory of international incomes, we use an aggregate production function with an intangible capital input as well as labor and tangible capital inputs. The per capita aggregate production function we use is simply

$$y_t = A(1 + \gamma)^{(1-\theta_k-\theta_z)t} k_t^{\theta_k} z_t^{\theta_z},$$

where $\theta_k + \theta_z < 1$ is capital's share. The economy's resource constraint is $c + x_k + x_z \leq y$, where x_k is investment in physical capital and x_z is investment in intangible capital. Labor and land share is $1 - \theta_k - \theta_z$. The capital stocks are assumed to evolve according to

$$k_{t+1} = (1 - \delta_k)k_t + x_{kt}$$

$$z_{t+1} = (1 - \delta_z)z_t + x_{zt}.$$

If savings rates are constant, that is, the ratios of investments to total product y are constant, this economy will converge to a steady-state growth path with all per capita variables growing at rate γ.

We will go through the calibration exercise in some detail because it is nonstandard. This is because investments in intangible capital are not reported in the NIPA data. What this means is that the NIPA data cannot be used to restrict the values of the intangible capital parameters θ_z and δ_z. It also means that reported factor income shares cannot be used in this calibration as they were in the calibration of the standard growth theory. Since there is unmeasured investment on the product side, there must be an equal amount of unreported income. Who receives this income is not clear. For non–firm-specific human capital, theory suggests that it is part of the income of the individual receiving the training. More generally, for firm-specific investments, theory provides little guidance as to how this income is divided among the firm's stakeholders.

We start the calibration by reorganizing the NIPA data according to this theoretical framework. One issue is how to deal with the government. On the product side, we set consumption equal to the sum of private and public consumption and tangible investment equal to the sum of private and public tangible investment. We treat the services of government capital (that is, the services of roads and government buildings) as an intermediate good to the business sector. The final adjustment is that we follow the United Nations rather than the United States NIPA system and assume that borrowers rather than lenders implicitly purchase the financial intermediation services. This reduces net interest income and consumption by equal amounts. With these adjustments, the statistics used in the calibration are a 0.20 ratio of investment to the NIPA GDP, a 5 percent real return, a physical capital to NIPA GDP ratio of 2.5, and a 2.0 percent real consumption growth rate.[12] These are the approximate averages for the United States in the last half of the twentieth century.

Given values for parameters θ_z and δ_z, the above observations together with steady-state conditions restrict the values of the other model parameters. The key issue in the calibration is how to restrict the values of θ_z and δ_z. Their values can be restricted using data on the size of investment in intangible capital and depreciation on this stock. As noted earlier, such data are not to be found in the national accounts since investments in intangible capital are expensed. Without such data, it is impossible to say with any precision what these quantities are. We can only provide broad estimates for their sizes. Our earlier calculations placed the size of investment in intangible capital in the United States to be between 30 percent and 50 percent of NIPA GDP. For depreciation, we think 2.5 percent is the lower bound for the depreciation rate, as there is both obsolescence and physical deterioration, the latter of which occurs as individuals exit the labor force.

While we cannot say what is the precise size of investment in intangible capital or what is the precise depreciation on this stock, it turns out that for the purpose at hand we do not have to. It suffices to calibrate the model to the high end of the plausible range of intangible capital investments setting the depreciation rate at the low end of its plausible range. If we find that for these values of θ_z and δ_z differences in savings rates do not give rise to differences in relative steady-state NIPA GDPs of the order of magnitude observed in the data, then we can conclude that the model cannot account for international income differences for any plausible values of θ_z and δ_z. The reason for this is as follows. Differences in savings rates have large consequences for steady-state relative NIPA GDPs only if capital's share is large. Large capital shares are implied by large capital-to-output ratios, which are implied by small depreciation rates and/or large investment ratios. By assuming the depreciation rate is at the lower end of its plausible range and using an intangible capital investment rate at the upper end of its plausible range, the calibrated value of θ_z is the highest plausible value. If the model fails for this value of θ_z, it fails to account for the huge disparity in international incomes for all plausible values of θ_z.

The following five necessary steady-state conditions are used in the calibration:

$$i + \delta_k = \theta_k A k^{(\theta_k - 1)} z^{\theta_z}$$

$$i + \delta_z = \theta_z A k^{\theta_k} z^{(\theta_z - 1)}$$

$$c + x_k + x_z = A k^{\theta_k} z^{\theta_z}$$

$$x_k = (\gamma + \delta_k)k$$

$$x_z = (\gamma + \delta_z)z.$$

The first two conditions are just the profit-maximizing conditions that marginal products equal rental prices. The rental price is the sum of the interest rate (denoted by i) plus the depreciation rate. The third is the aggregate production function with the economy's resource constraint. The last two are the conditions that investment is such that per capita stocks grow at rate γ. Per capita capital stocks, consumption, and investments in the above five necessary steady-state conditions have all been divided by $(1 + \gamma)^t$.

Normalizing NIPA output to 1, the observations to which the model is calibrated are $x_k = 0.20$, $c = 0.80$, $k = 2.50$, $i = 0.05$, $\Delta y / y = 0.02$, and $x_z = 0.50$. Using these data and the assumption that $\delta_z = 0.025$, the above five necessary steady-state conditions determine the parameters, $(\theta_z, \delta_k, \theta_k, A)$, as well as the steady-state intangible capital stock, z. From these conditions we arrive at $\theta_z = 0.56$, $\delta_k = 0.06$, $\theta_k = 0.18$, and $z = 11.11$.

Now that we have calibrated the model we can ask whether adding intangible capital to the neoclassical growth model makes it a theory of international incomes. It is, if plausible differences in savings rates give rise to large differences in relative steady-state NIPA GDP levels of the order of magnitude observed across countries. We therefore consider lower intangible capital savings rates, $x_z/(c + x_k)$, and solve for relative steady-state NIPA GDPs. In doing so, we allow the return on intangible capital in a country to differ from the return in the United States. However, we do require that the return on physical capital be the same across countries. This we do because savings rates, $x_k/(c + x_k)$, do not differ systematically across rich and poor countries as reported in table 3.2.

Table 3.3 summarizes these results. The steady-state effects of lower investment rates in intangible capital are not small. As can be seen from the table, if the investment rate in intangible capital in one country is 1/8 the U.S. rate, that country will have a steady-state NIPA GDP that is 4 percent of the U.S. level. This is approximately the difference in income livings between the poorest countries in

Table 3.3
Effects of a lower intangible capital investment rate on steady-state GDP and intangible capital return

Intangible capital investment rate $x_z/(c + x_k)$	Relative GDP $(c + x_k)$	Return on intangible capital investment x_z
0.500	1.00	5%
0.250	0.45	10%
0.125	0.15	20%
0.063	0.04	40%

the world and the United States. In this respect, the results seem promising. However, such a saving rate difference implies a rate of return of 40 percent in the poor country. A 20 percent rate of return in our view is at the upper end of plausibility. Saving rate differences cannot be this large.

Lowering the value of θ_z by assuming a higher depreciation rate or by using a lower estimate for unmeasured investment does not change the conclusion of the analysis. For differences in investment rates that are large enough to generate differences in NIPA outputs of the magnitude observed in the data, the implied returns to intangible investment are implausibly large. We conclude that the intangible capital extension of the neoclassical growth model with no differences in TFP is not a model of international income differences.

4   Growth Theory with a Human Capital Sector

In the last chapter, we discussed the quantitative implications of a multisector model for international income differences. We showed that if capital-labor ratios are approximately the same across sectors, the single-sector and multisector models behave essentially the same way, at least relative to the development issues being addressed here. If the capital goods producing sector is highly capital intensive, however, differences in savings rates will have large level effects. Rebelo's (1991) endogenous growth model establishes this result. As a matter of fact, the sector producing physical capital is not highly capital intensive. However, the sector producing human capital is highly intensive in the human capital input. This observation is probably what led Lucas (1988) to add a nonmarket, human capital producing sector, which is intensive in the human capital input. In a model with a human capital producing sector, differences in savings rates appropriately defined might have large consequences for steady-state levels of income.

In this chapter, we explore this issue using a variant of the Lucas (1988) model that focuses on training that increases the units of labor services an individual can supply per unit of time allocated to the market sector. The model differs from that of Lucas in that savings rates determine relative steady-state income levels and not growth rates. Another difference is in the definition of human capital. Our definition is narrower than the one employed by Lucas. However, it is consistent with the definition used by some development economists who view differences in the investment in education and training as the source of most of the differences in international incomes.[13]

Human Capital Sector Model Extension

In the model economy we study, individuals allocate some fraction of their time s_h to enhancing their human capital and the remainder $1 - s_h$ to market production. There is a standard neoclassical production technology for the consumption and tangible capital production function, namely,

$$y_t = A k_t^\theta [(1 - s_{ht}) h_t]^{(1-\theta)} \tag{4.1}$$

where $(1 - s_{ht})h_t$ is human capital services allocated to the production of market goods.[14] The resource constraint for this economy is $c_t + x_{kt} \leq y_t$, and the law of motion for tangible capital is

$$k_{t+1} = x_{kt} + (1 - \delta_k)k_t. \tag{4.2}$$

The key sector is the human capital production sector, which has the following production function:[15]

$$h_{t+1} - (1 - \delta_h)h_t = (1 + \gamma)^{(1-\sigma)t}(s_{ht}h_t)^\sigma. \tag{4.3}$$

In (4.3), δ_h is the depreciation rate for human capital and σ is a parameter that determines how intensive human capital is in the production of human capital. As is evident from (4.3), the production of human capital is subject to exogenous technological change. On account of this exogenous technological change, there is sustained growth in per worker output that is independent of a country's savings rate. The idea that growth in useable knowledge leads to higher returns on the investment in human capital is, we think, a plausible one. The knowledge acquired per unit of time is greater if the stock of publicly available knowledge is larger. The information in a library today surely exceeds that contained in libraries 100 years ago. The amount of knowledge an individual can acquire in an hour's time in a library today is surely higher than the amount he could acquire in an hour 100 years ago.

Savings Rates and Steady-State Relative Income

A constant savings rate policy in this world is defined as one for which both the fraction of human capital allocated to human capital production s_h and the physical capital savings rate $s_k = x_k/y$ are constant. The steady-state growth rate of an economy with these production technologies is γ for any constant savings rate policy. The key parameter for determining how the fraction of time allocated to human capital investment affects steady-state output is σ, the exponent in the human capital production function. If it is sufficiently near one, any given difference in the savings rate s_h leads to arbitrarily large differences in steady-state outputs.

This model can be calibrated to the U.S. growth facts, given values for the human capital depreciation rate δ_h and the curvature parameter σ in the human capital production function. The results are not sensitive to the value of δ_h selected; therefore, we simply select $\delta_h = \delta_k$. As the results, however, are sensitive to the value of σ selected, the model is calibrated for a number of values of σ to determine if for any value of σ the implications of the model are plausible. For values of σ for which the implications of the model are not inconsistent with measurement, we explore the consequences of differences in human capital investment rates for relative steady-state income.

The set of observations used in the calibration is the same as the one used in the calibration of the intangible capital model of chapter 3. More specifically, normalizing NIPA GDP to 1, we have $x_k = 0.20, c = 0.80, i = 0.05$, and $\Delta y/y = 0.02$. Unlike the intangible capital model of chapter 3, market output in this model corresponds to NIPA GDP. Using these data, the assumed value of σ, and the assumption that $\delta_h = \delta_k = \delta$, the parameters (θ, δ, A) and the variables (h, s_h) can be solved for using equations (4.1)–(4.3) and the conditions that the returns on physical and human capital investment equal the interest rate. These return conditions are

$$i_{t-1} = \theta A k_t^{\theta-1}[(1 - s_{ht})h_t]^{\theta-1} - \delta_k$$

$$i_{t-1} = \sigma(s_{ht}h_t)^{\sigma-1} - \delta_h.$$

Table 4.1 reports s_h, the fraction of time allocated to human capital investment, for selected values of σ. As can be seen, the larger is σ, the larger is this fraction. For

Table 4.1
Implied time allocated to human capital investment for different σ

Value of σ	Implied fraction of time s_h
0.00	0.00
0.20	0.16
0.30	0.24
0.40	0.32
0.60	0.48
0.80	0.64
0.90	0.72

values of σ greater than 0.60, as much time is allocated to training as is allocated to market production. Such numbers are well in excess of the numbers reported in time allocation studies. We conclude from this exercise that values of $\sigma > 0.60$ are implausible.

The question now addressed is whether variations in s_h can account for the large differences in international incomes for any plausible value of σ. To address this question, we consider reductions in s_h. In doing so, we allow the return on human capital in a country to differ from the return on human capital in the United States. The returns on physical capital are not allowed to differ. Table 4.2 summarizes the results of these numerical exercises. The table reports steady-state income and returns on human capital investment as a function of s_h for two values of σ.

If $\sigma = 0.30$, differences in the time allocated to human capital production imply small differences in steady-state outputs. For this value of σ, if the fraction of time allocated

Table 4.2
Effects of time allocated to human capital investment on steady-state output

$\sigma = 0.30$		
Fraction of time s_h	Relative GDP	Return on h investment
0.24	1.00	5%
0.12	0.86	15%
0.06	0.76	35%
$\sigma = 0.60$		
Fraction of time s_h	Relative GDP	Return on h investment
0.48	1.00	5%
0.24	0.52	15%
0.12	0.21	35%

to human capital production is reduced from 0.24 to 0.06, output decreases by a factor of only 1.3. If $\sigma = 0.60$, the effects of differences in the time allocated to producing human capital are larger, but still small relative to the data. For this value of σ, a reduction in the time allocated to human capital production from 0.48 to 0.06 decreases output by a factor of only 5. Clearly, this model cannot account for the huge observed disparity in international incomes.

Another problem for this theory is that such large reductions in s_h imply implausibly high returns on human capital investment, nearly 35 percent in the poorest countries compared to only 5 percent in the richest countries. With such high returns on human capital investment in poor countries, human capital should flow from the rich to the poor countries. In fact, the flow tends to be in the opposite direction.

The conclusion of this analysis is that adding a human capital production sector to the neoclassical model fails to make that theory a theory of international income differences. The problem lies with the technology side, not the preference side. Specifically, the problem is the assumption that countries share a common total factor productivity (TFP). We next turn to some direct evidence of the limited importance of schooling for international income differences.

Direct Evidence of Human Capital's Role

Hall and Jones (1999) provide direct evidence against this human capital theory of output differences. More precisely, they find that the technology parameter in this theory differs across countries and is strongly and positively associated with the level of development. Their procedure is as follows. They construct measures of human capital services and physical capital services for a large set of countries. They then take these measures and for each country estimate the TFP implied by the theory.

Their measure of human capital is based on average years of schooling of the population aged twenty-five and over. They construct this measure by treating individuals with different years of schooling as providing different types of human capital services. Each type of service is multiplied by its rental price, and these values are aggregated over all types in the population to obtain the aggregate of human capital services. This is the same aggregation principle that underlies the output side of the NIPA. The rental prices for each type of human capital service are taken from wage equations estimated by Mincer (1994).

Hall and Jones (1999) ignore experience in constructing their measure of human capital services. Experience is an important variable in these empirical wage equations. For their purpose, however, ignoring this factor is reasonable, because work experience differs little across countries.[16]

Physical capital services are measured by each country's physical capital stock. Physical capital stocks are computed from the PWT5.6 investment data using the perpetual inventory method. We have already discussed several potential problems with this method for the purpose of making cross-country comparisons. Most notably, useful lives are probably longer in poor countries given that the price of maintenance is lower there (Heston and Summers 1996). Consequently, physical capital stocks in the poor countries are surely underestimated and TFPs overestimated in the Hall and Jones (1999) analysis.

Using output per worker from the PWT5.6 and their physical and human capital measures for 127 countries,

Hall and Jones (1999) compute the TFP implied by the theory. Due to data limitations, they ignore differences in hours worked per adult across countries. This, however, is not a problem for their analysis because these differences are of second or third order in importance.

Hall and Jones (1999) find significant differences in TFP that are strongly and positively related to the level of development. They report a correlation coefficient between the log of TFP and the log of output per worker equal to 0.89. Table 4.3 presents a representative sample of their findings for some large benchmarked rich, middle income, and poor countries. The difference in TFP implied by this theory between the rich and the middle income is of the order of 2. Between the rich and the poor, the factor difference is between 4 and 6.

Another important piece of direct evidence we present against a human capital theory of international incomes

Table 4.3
Implied TFP differences, 1988

Country	Per worker output	Relative TFP
United States	1.00	1.00
West Germany	.82	.91
France	.82	1.13
United Kingdom	.73	1.01
Japan	.59	.66
South Korea	.38	.58
Portugal	.37	.75
Malaysia	.27	.45
Thailand	.16	.37
Philippines	.13	.22
India	.09	.27
Kenya	.06	.17

Source: Hall and Jones 1999.

derives from studies of relative productivity among the large rich countries in a variety of industries. The United States is overall the world's most productive nation. It has been since 1890, when it overtook the United Kingdom. However, the United States is not the most productive nation in all industries in all sectors. While value added per worker in service sector industries is uniformly higher in the United States, it is not uniformly higher in manufacturing sector industries. In that sector, Japan is more productive than the United States in a number of important industries, including the auto and steel industries.

Table 4.4 presents some estimates of value added per worker in a selected set of manufacturing and service

Table 4.4
Relative value added per worker: Germany, Japan, and the United States

Manufacturer's industries		
Industry	Japan	Germany
Automobiles	116	66
Automobile parts	124	76
Metal working	119	100
Steel	145	100
Computer	95	89
Consumer electronics	115	62
Food	33	76
Beer	69	44
Soap and detergent	94	76

Service center industries				
Industry	Japan	Germany	U.K.	France
Retailing	44	96	82	69
Telecommunications	66	50	38	56
Banking	—	68	64	—

Source: Baily 1993; Baily and Gersbach 1995.

industries in a number of large rich countries. All productivity levels are expressed relative to the U.S. level, which have been normalized to 100. The estimates are from Baily (1993) and Baily and Gersbach (1995).[17] As table 4.4 shows, industry value added per worker varies a lot among the large rich countries—by a factor as big as 3 in some industries. They also report that physical capital per worker in each industry differs very little across these countries.

Why do we see these large differences as evidence against a schooling capital theory of international incomes? The reason is rather simple. There was no important difference in the schooling of the workforce across industries within a given country. Consequently, if schooling capital differences were the key to understanding income differences, then one country should be the most productive in all industries, and not just a few. This and the other evidence presented in this chapter suggest that we look to something other than human capital to explain international income differences. In particular, they suggest we look to differences in TFP.

5   Growth Theory with TFP Differences

The previous two chapters considered whether differences in savings rates account for the differences in international incomes. We found that even when capital is defined broadly to include both physical and intangible varieties, differences in savings rates can at most account for only a small part of the observed differences in international incomes. This failure leads us to consider differences in total factor productivity (TFP). In this chapter we modify the growth theory by permitting international differences in TFP and then explore the implications of the resulting theory. We emphasize that while we permit TFP to differ across countries, we do not abandon the principle of a common technology across countries, without which there would be little if any discipline to the analysis. This may seem contradictory, but it is not. As we show in the next chapter, policy differences with a common technology lead to TFP differences.

The size of capital's share has important implications for the size of the relative steady-state income difference associated with any given relative TFP difference. As seen in chapter 3, relative steady-state income levels are proportional to relative TFP levels raised to the power $1/(1 - \theta)$, where θ is the sum of the physical capital share parameter and the intangible capital share. If θ is small, large differences in TFP are needed to account for the observed differences in incomes. Solow (1957), who abstracted from intangible capital, had a capital-share parameter near 0.25. With this capital-share parameter, TFP must differ by a factor of 12 to generate a factor difference in relative income levels of 27, which is roughly the difference between the richest and poorest countries in the world. On the other hand, if this capital share parameter is 0.75, TFPs need differ by only a factor of 2.3 to account for this difference in relative income levels. Factor differences in TFP of 3 are reasonable across countries—differences of 12 are not. Consequently, one test of the theory is whether the total capital share parameter θ is reasonably large.

The size of capital's share also has implications for the speed of convergence to the balanced growth path. If θ is small, convergence to the balanced growth path is fast, while if θ is large, convergence is slow. This is the property of the model we shall exploit in this chapter to narrow the range of values for capital's share. A country will be below its balanced growth path following an increase in its TFP, which as we shall show in the next chapter follows improvements in policy. This leads us to search for a natural experiment where a country experienced an important, relatively permanent change in its political-economic institutions and where, subsequently, the economy of that country began to converge to a significantly higher balanced growth path.

Japan, subsequent to its recovery from World War II, provides an almost ideal natural experiment for our purposes. Figure 5.1 shows the Japanese development experience over the last century. Prior to World War II, Japan's economy was following a balanced growth path at about 25 percent of the industrial leader, which was then and

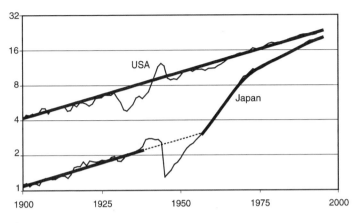

Figure 5.1
Trends in output per capita, 1900–1995 (thousands of 1990 U.S. $)
Source: Summers and Heston 1991; Maddison 1995 before 1950.

continues to be the United States. Following Japan's defeat in the war, the occupying American military forces imposed major changes in Japan's political and economic institutions. Subsequent to the implementation of these changes, the Japanese economy recovered quickly from the war disruptions, and by 1957 the Japanese economy was again at 25 percent of the industrial leader. Given this highly successful recovery, it seems reasonable to assume that the Japanese people expected the outside, imposed changes to persist with only minor changes for the indefinite future. Thus, Japan satisfies our first requirement.

The second requirement for our natural experiment is also met—namely, that the economy subsequent to the changes in its economic institutions began to converge to a much higher balanced growth path. In the 1957–1969 period per capita GDP increased from 25 percent of the leader to 50 percent of the leader according to the PWT5.6. This catching up was not the result of the leader, which was the United States during this period, slowing down. Indeed, U.S. per capita GDP grew by 60 percent in this period. The Japanese economy in this period is a dramatic example of catching up. As can be seen in figure 5.1, the new balanced growth path is close to that of the industrial leader.

The exact nature of the quantitative analysis that we conduct in this chapter is as follows. To begin, we restrict the model parameters by using both the Japanese non–steady-state observation and U.S. steady-state observations. We calibrate the non–steady-state behavior of the model to the Japanese postwar development experience and the balanced growth path behavior of the model to the U.S. postwar experience. In a sense, the calibration serves to test the model along two important dimensions. We then proceed to test whether the theory can account for the huge observed disparity in international incomes. This we do by determining the relative steady-state per capita NIPA GDP associated with a given relative difference in TFP for the capital share implied by the first two tests. We find that these differences are quite plausible.

Because we need to analyze the transitional dynamics of the model, we can no longer abstract from optimal capital accumulation where consumers equate intertemporal rates of substitution. This is to say that we can no longer assume a fixed savings rate as we did in the previous two chapters. When the analysis is limited to steady-state comparisons, this assumption does not matter. It does not matter because with optimal capital accumulation a country's savings rate is constant along its balanced growth path and is independent of the country's level of TFP. This is not the case for the balanced growth path with optimal accumulation. What this means is that we must explicitly model the preference side of the economy. In being explicit, we must also allow for a labor/leisure decision, as the speed of convergence to the new balanced growth path depends on whether agents can substitute leisure and labor.

The Model

Business Sector

We begin with the per worker aggregate production function that we studied in chapter 3. We modify it so that TFP, denoted by A, is specific to each country and so that it includes the amount of time (workweek), h_t, that workers operate the capital. The output per worker of a firm that is operated an h_t length workweek and uses k_t units of physical capital per worker and z_t units of intangible capital per worker is

$$y_t = Ah_t(1 + \gamma)^{(1-\theta_z-\theta_k)t}k_t^{\theta_k}z_t^{\theta_z}. \tag{5.1}$$

Per worker output being proportional to the length of the workweek does not lead to increasing returns to scale. In fact, there are constant returns to scale with this technological assumption. Doubling all inputs means doubling the number of people working workweek h_t as well as doubling the aggregate quantities of the two types of capital. Consequently, doubling all inputs doubles the maximum possible output. Replication implies that there are constant returns to scale with this technology.

We assume that a firm owns its intangible capital. This we do because much of the intangible capital we identified in chapter 3 is embodied in firms and groups of individuals rather than specific individuals. Given there are constant returns to scale, we can and will proceed as if there were a single price taking firm. The firm increases its stock of intangible capital by making investments. The firm's intangible capital evolves according to the following equation:

$$z_{t+1} = (1 - \delta_z)z_t + x_{zt}. \tag{5.2}$$

Tangible capital k_t, in contrast, is rented from households. The firm's dividend at date t is

$$v_{ft} \equiv y_t - w_t(h_t) - r_{kt}k_t - x_{zt}. \tag{5.3}$$

In (5.3), $w_t(h)$ is a function that gives the real rental price at date t of a worker who works an h hour workweek and r_{kt} is the real rental price of physical capital at date t. The reason w is a function of h is that workweeks of different lengths are interpreted as different commodities. Thus, there is a real rental price for each length workweek. It turns out that in equilibrium all individuals work the same workweek length, and consequently, the market clearing quantities of all other workweek lengths are zero. Finally, if $v_{ft} > 0$, the firm is paying a dividend to holders of equity, and if $v_{ft} < 0$, the firm is issuing new equity.

Because the firm owns its stock of intangible capital, the relevant maximization problem is dynamic rather than static. The problem facing the firm is to maximize the present value of its dividends,

$$V(z_0) \equiv \max \sum_{t=0}^{\infty} p_t v_{ft}, \tag{5.4}$$

subject to constraints (5.1), (5.2), and (5.3). Here, $\{p_t\}$ is the sequence of Arrow-Debreu prices of the composite commodity. In maximizing (5.4), the firm takes the prices, $\{p_t, w_t(h), r_{kt}\}_{t=0}^{\infty}$, as given.

Household Sector

Since we are analyzing the transitional dynamics and thus require capital accumulation to be optimal, we need to be explicit about household preferences and endowments. For similar reasons, we cannot abstract from the labor/leisure decision. We introduce leisure to preferences in the standard way. The discounted utility stream of a household over its infinite lifetime is

$$\sum_{t=0}^{\infty} \beta^t [\ln(c_t) + \phi \ln(1 - h_t)], \tag{5.5}$$

where c_t denotes the consumption good at time t and $1 - h_t$ denotes leisure at date t. The parameter β is the subjective time discount factor, and the parameter ϕ is the expenditure share parameter. The parameters satisfy $\phi > 0$, and $0 < \beta < 1$.

Each household at each date divides its one unit endowment of productive time between leisure and labor. At date 0, households are endowed with physical capital. All households have the same initial endowment of physical capital and have equal claims to the dividends of firms. The law of motion for the stock of physical capital is

$$k_{t+1} = (1 - \delta_k)k_t + x_{kt}. \tag{5.6}$$

Physical capital is rented to firms and generates physical capital income $r_{kt}k_t$.[18] At date t, a household which works an h_t hour workweek also receives labor income equal to $w_t(h_t)$ and dividends from firms v_{ft}.

The problem of the household is to maximize (5.5) subject to the household physical capital constraints (5.6) and subject to the household's budget constraint

$$\sum_{t=0}^{\infty} p_t[c_t + x_{kt}] \leq \sum_{t=0}^{\infty} p_t[w_t(h_t) + r_{kt}k_t + v_{ft}]. \tag{5.7}$$

The household, like the firm, takes prices $\{p_t, w_t(h), r_{kt}\}_{t=0}^{\infty}$ as given.

Equilibrium

The following set of equations, along with equations (5.1), (5.2), (5.3), and (5.6) and the transversality condition, are necessary and sufficient conditions for a competitive equilibrium:

$$i_t \equiv \frac{p_t}{p_{t+1}} - 1 \tag{5.8}$$

$$r_{kt} = i_{t-1} + \delta_k \tag{5.9}$$

$$r_{zt} \equiv i_{t-1} + \delta_z \tag{5.10}$$

$$r_{kt}k_t = \theta_k y_t \tag{5.11}$$

$$r_{zt}z_t = \theta_z y_t \tag{5.12}$$

$$w_t(h_t) = (1 - \theta_k - \theta_z)y_t \tag{5.13}$$

$$\frac{c_{t+1}}{c_t} = \beta(1 + i_t) \tag{5.14}$$

$$\frac{\phi c_t}{1 - h_t} = w_t'(h_t) = \frac{y_t}{h_t} \tag{5.15}$$

$$c_t + x_{kt} = y_t - x_{zt}. \tag{5.16}$$

Equation (5.8) is the definition of the interest rate. From the household's maximization problem, (5.9) is the rental price of physical capital. Equation (5.10) is the implicit rental price of z. Equations (5.11) and (5.12) follow from the firm's maximization of the present value of dividends. Equation (5.13) follows from aggregate constant returns. Equation (5.14) and the first equality in equation (5.15) follow from the household's maximization problem. The second equality in (5.15) exploits the fact that the derivative at h_t of the firm's reservation demand for workweeks of different lengths h is y_t / h_t. Equation (5.16) is the goods market clearing condition.

Balanced Growth

Along the balanced growth path, per capita output $\{y_t\}$, per capita expenditure categories $\{c_t, x_{kt}, x_{zt}\}$, per capita capital stocks $\{k_t, z_t\}$, and per capita income categories $\{w_t(h_t), r_{kt}k_t, v_{ft}\}$ all grow at the same rate. This growth rate is equal to γ.

Model Calibration

The difficulty we faced in calibrating the two-capital extension of the growth model without differences in TFP persists here. Namely, the NIPA data are of no use in restricting the value of intangible capital parameters, δ_z and θ_z, since most investments in intangible capital are expensed in the NIPA. The explicit treatment of preferences does not make the calibration more difficult. Given values of δ_z and θ_z, all the other model parameters, including the preference parameters, β and ϕ, are tied down by the U.S. steady-state growth observation used in the chapter 3 calibration and the observation for the time allocated to market work in the United States. Normalizing NIPA GDP to 1, the U.S. observations used in the calibration are $x_k = 0.20, k = 2.50, i = .05, \Delta y/y = .02$, and $h = .40$. The fraction of time allocated to the market, h, is the workweek divided by 100, because people have about 100 hours of nonsleeping and personal care time per week. Given values for δ_z and θ_z and the above U.S. observations, equations (5.1), (5.2), (5.6), and (5.8)–(5.16) can be used to solve for all the other parameter values as well as the variables x_z and z.

To tie down values for δ_z and θ_z we use the Japanese development experience over the postwar period as well as our estimates of the fraction of unmeasured investment to NIPA GDP in the economy. As noted in chapter 3, their size could be anywhere from 30 percent to 50 percent of NIPA GDP with our best-guess estimate being in the upper end of the range. For any given amount of unmeasured investment, exact values of δ_z and θ_z can be determined that match the transitional dynamics of the model to the Japanese development experience. This experience shows an increase in per capita output from 25 percent of the leader to 50 percent of the leader over a twelve-year period.

In calculating the transitional path of the model economy, we assume the beginning period capital stocks for which the beginning period per capita GDP in Japan relative to the United States and the model relative to steady state match. In choosing the capital stocks, we assume an initial mix of physical and intangible capital so that the nonnegativity of investment conditions are not binding in the initial period. In no case that we considered was the nonnegativity of investment conditions binding at any point along the path. In calculating this path, we also assume that TFP in Japan and the United States are the same over this period. This we do because the data suggest that Japan up until the early 1970s was converging to the U.S. balanced growth path. Results are not overly sensitive to the assumption that TFP in Japan and the United States are equal.

Findings

The important finding is that for any amount of unmeasured investment in the range of 30 percent to 50 percent of NIPA GDP, the total capital share, $\theta_k + \theta_z$, must be large for an economy to move from 25 percent of the balanced growth path to 50 percent in twelve years. The calibrated total capital share, $\theta_k + \theta_z$, ranges from 0.67 to 0.70. Of these values, only capital shares close to 0.70 are reasonable. For $\theta_k + \theta_z = 0.70$, the calibrated depreciation rate, δ_z, is 0.035, which is near the low end of the reasonable range for this parameter, and the size of unmeasured investment, $x_z/(c + x_k)$, is 0.50, which is near the upper end of the reasonable range for such investment. For smaller values of $\theta_k + \theta_z$ consistent with the Japanese development experience, the depreciation rate is smaller, and for larger values of $\theta_k + \theta_z$ consistent with the Japanese development experience, unmeasured investment is larger.

Figure 5.2 plots the path of the model economy and the path of Japanese output per equivalent adult (RGDPEA in the PWT5.6) associated with $\theta_k + \theta_z = 0.70$. The fact that the model and data are so close prior to 1974 is a confirmation of the prediction of the theory. The fact that there is a divergence subsequent to 1974 is not surprising. In 1974 there was an oil crisis that may well have precipitated changes in the Japanese economy with the partial reemergence of the bureaucratic-industrial complex that characterized the prewar Japanese economy. Such a change could well have reduced the efficiency of the Japanese economy and lowered its steady-state growth path.

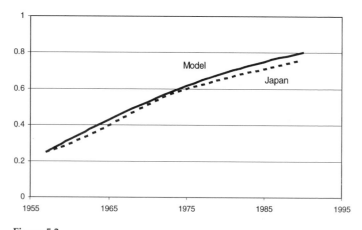

Figure 5.2
Model versus Japanese development: Fraction of leader, 1957–1990
Source: Summers and Heston 1991.

Despite the success of the theory, there are reasons to believe our estimate of 0.70 for total capital's share is probably a little high. First, one dimension of the data the model does not match precisely is the decline in hours worked per person in Japan. In the model, hours worked per person decrease by 10 percent as per capita output goes from 25 percent to 50 percent of steady-state levels over twelve years. In Japan, hours worked per person decreased by only 8 percent between 1957 and 1969. If the model were modified to match the actual decline in hours worked per worker in Japan, then total capital's share would become a little lower. The reason is that, holding other things equal, a smaller decline in hours implies a slower convergence rate. Therefore, to compensate, the capital share must be lowered.

A second reason we think total capital's share is probably too high is that we abstracted from consumer durable

Table 5.1
Relative TFP and output

Relative TFP A	Relative NIPA GDP $c + x_k$
1.00	1.00
0.50	0.13
0.33	0.04

accumulation by households. The adjustment to capital's share will be small because consumer durables are only about 10 percent of the physical capital stock, which is smaller than the intangible capital stock. Nonetheless, introducing consumer durable accumulation would slow down convergence and necessitate a lower total capital share. It would also result in a smaller estimate for unmeasured investment and a higher estimate for δ_z. Given these considerations, we will use a number of 2/3 for $\theta_k + \theta_z$ in examining the implications of the theory for steady-state output differences.

Steady-State Output and TFP Differences

We now examine the implications of our theory for international income differences. In particular, we analyze how relative steady-state income levels in the calibrated model depend on relative TFP, A. Table 5.1 reports the relative steady-state output levels implied by a given relative TFP for a value of $\theta_k + \theta_z = 2/3$.

The factor difference in relative steady-state per capita output associated with a given relative TFP difference A equals $A^{1/(1-\theta_k-\theta_z)}$. Thus, for a total capital share equal to 2/3, relative steady-state output differences equal A^3 for relative TFP difference, A. Consequently, a country with a

TFP level that is 1/3 the U.S. level has a relative steady-state income level that is roughly 1/27 that of the United States. This is roughly the difference in incomes between the United States and the poorest countries in the world. A factor difference in TFP of 3 is plausible.

For countries whose incomes relative to U.S. income stayed more or less constant over the 1950–1988 period, the model with $\theta_z + \theta_k = 2/3$ has the following implication for the size of those countries' relative TFP. For the United Kingdom, which maintained an income level relative to the U.S. level of roughly 60 percent over the 1950–1988 period, the model implies TFP that was 86 percent of the U.S. level. For Colombia, which maintained a relative income of roughly 22 percent of the U.S. level, the model implies TFP 64 percent of the U.S. level. For Paraguay, which maintained a relative income of roughly 16 percent over the 1950–1988 period, the implied TFP is 59 percent of the U.S. level, while for Pakistan, which maintained a relative income of roughly 10 percent of the U.S. level, the implied TFP is 51 percent.

We conclude that the neoclassical growth theory with differences in TFP and with intangible capital accounts well for the behavior of international income differences at a point in time and over time. The model matches the development miracle of Japan. It matches the U.S. growth observations, and it gives rise to large differences in relative incomes for modest differences in relative TFP.

6   Constraints on Firm Technologies and TFP

In chapter 5, we found that the neoclassical growth model with unmeasured investment accounts well for countries' growth and development given the behavior of these countries' total factor productivity (TFP). In this model, individuals make investments up to the point at which rates of return are roughly equal across countries. The nature of the tax system does affect individuals' savings and does lead to some differences in the amount of capital accumulated. But tax rate differences are a minor factor in accounting for differences in international income and the development experiences of countries over time, because savings rates do not vary systematically with countries' incomes.

For the growth model to be a theory of development, however, it must be augmented by a theory of how policy differences lead to TFP differences. It cannot attribute these differences in TFP to differences in the stock of useable knowledge from which each country can draw. The stock of useable knowledge is something that is common across countries. Some other factor, or set of factors, must give rise to TFP differences.

These considerations lead us to focus on the theory underlying the aggregate production function and how policy can affect this function. This necessitates a modification in the definition of an aggregate production function. The standard textbook definition is the maximum output that can be produced given the quantities of the aggregate inputs. Our modified definition is the maximum output that can be produced given not only the technology constraints but also the constraints on the use of technologies arising from policies. As policies can differ across countries, the aggregate production function can differ even though there is a common world technology. Thus, with our framework, policy affects TFP by imposing or inducing constraints on the technologies that can be used as well as on how they are used.

In this chapter, we describe a plant technology along with constraints on its use that differ across countries that give rise to differences in TFP across countries. We consider the profit-maximization problem of the plant operator and then aggregate over plants to obtain the neoclassical production function analyzed in chapter 5 with differences in TFP. The plant technology we describe is based upon Parente and Prescott (1994). The policy we model is motivated by DeSoto's (1989) study of regulatory constraints in Peru. He reports that the nature of the regulatory system makes it extremely expensive to set up a new firm. He documents that an individual must obtain eleven separate permits, a process that can take more than 250 working days and requires that bribes be made. In New York City, in contrast, this process takes only two hours and requires that no bribes be made.

The Plant Technology and the Barrier

The production unit in the economy is a plant. A given number of workers, $\bar{N}$, are needed to operate a plant. The output of a plant depends on the number of hours the plant is operated, h_t, and the amount of physical capital the plant rents, K_t. Output also depends on the quality of the production unit. A plant's quality is denoted by B_t. Output is given by the following technology:

$$Y_t = \bar{N}h_t B_t K_t^{\theta_k}, \qquad 0 < \theta_k < 1. \tag{6.1}$$

There are no aggregate increasing returns to scale in our economy. The commodity space has many commodities. Workweeks of different lengths are different commodities, and plants with different qualities are different types of capital. Thus, there is a continuum of different types of both labor and technology capital inputs.[19] Given certain restrictions on technology parameters, there is an optimal plant size, and it is small relative to the economy. As the size of the economy increases, the number rather than the size of plants adjusts. A proportional increase in all inputs results in the same proportional increase in the number of plants and aggregate output. In the aggregate, then, there are constant returns to scale. As in the neoclassical model, the aggregate production possibility set is a convex cone.

To enhance its quality, a plant must make an investment of resources. Let $X_{BB'}$ denote the amount of investment a plant needs to make to enhance its quality from B to B' given barrier level π. There are several properties that the investment function should possess. First, the size of this investment increases with the size of the quality enhancement to be obtained; that is, $\partial X/\partial B' > 0$ and $\partial X/\partial B < 0$. Second, investment is subject to diminishing returns: $\partial^2 X/\partial B'^2 < 0$. Third, investment is additively separable in the sense that the amount of investment needed to advance the plant's quality from B to B' is the same amount needed to advance the plant's quality first from B to B^* and then from B^* to B'; that is, $X_{BB^*} + X_{B^*B'} = X_{BB'}$.

Fourth, for the same amount of investment, a plant with a currently lower quality realizes a larger increase in quality than a second plant that starts off with a higher quality, although the second plant still maintains a quality advantage. This feature is not independent of the first three properties of the investment function. The last and most important feature is that $X_{BB'}$ is increasing the size of the barrier π.

These features are implied by the function specified below that gives the amount of investment needed to advance a plant's quality from B to B' between dates t and $t + 1$:

$$X_{BB'} = (1 + \pi) \int_B^{B'} (S/W_t)^\alpha \, ds. \tag{6.2}$$

The parameter $\pi \geq 0$ represents the barriers to technology adoption in the country in which the plant is located. Barriers are country-specific and, in the spirit of DeSoto (1989), reflect policy distortions that add to the amount of resources needed to advance the plant's quality. As we shall show later in this chapter, barriers give rise to differences in TFP at the aggregate level. The variable W represents the stock of useable knowledge in the world. This variable includes the stock of blueprints, ideas, and scientific principles, among other things. This world knowledge is available to all plants in the world. In effect, useable knowledge spills over to the entire world instantaneously.[20] We assume that world knowledge grows at the constant rate of $\gamma_W > 0$.[21] Thus,

$$W_{t+1} = W_0(1 + \gamma_W)^t. \tag{6.3}$$

The effect of this growth in world knowledge is to decrease the amount of investment required to advance a plant's quality by a given amount. Effectively, $\partial X / \partial W < 0$. The idea behind this assumption is rather intuitive: with advances in world knowledge, fewer resources are required to advance a plant's quality. This feature helps generate the outcome that development rates increase over time, holding development levels and barriers fixed.

For the purpose at hand, it is useful to integrate (6.2) and make a change in variables. Integration of (6.2) implies that

$$(\alpha + 1)X_{BB'} = (1 + \pi)\frac{B_{t+1}^{\alpha+1} - B_t^{\alpha+1}}{W_t^\alpha}. \tag{6.4}$$

Define

$$Z_t \equiv \frac{(1 + \pi)B_t^{\alpha+1}}{(1 + \alpha)W_{t-1}^\alpha}. \tag{6.5}$$

Variable Z has the economic interpretation of the value of the sum of a plant's past investments in quality improvement. In other words, Z is a plant's intangible capital stock. In this representation, the stock of date t intangible capital, Z_t, is measured in terms of the date t composite-output good, Y_t. This can be seen more readily by defining $X_Z \equiv X_{BB'}$, $\theta_z \equiv 1/(1 + \alpha)$, $(1 - \delta_z) \equiv 1/(1 + \gamma_w)^{(1-\theta_z)/\theta_z}$, and $(1 + \gamma)^{(1-\theta_z-\theta_k)} \equiv (1 + \gamma_W)^{(1-\theta_z)}$. With the appropriate change in variables, the investment equation (6.4) becomes

$$Z_{t+1} = (1 - \delta_z)Z_t + X_{zt}, \tag{6.6}$$

and the plant technology equation (6.1) becomes

$$Y_t = \mu(1 + \pi)^{-\theta_z}h_t(1 + \gamma)^{(1-\theta_z-\theta_k)t}\bar{N}K_t^{\theta_k}Z_t^{\theta_z}. \tag{6.7}$$

In (6.7), μ is a constant that depends on W_0, γ_W, and θ_z and so does not differ across countries. Notice that with this change of variables, the plant technology appears to be characterized by exogenous technological change. It is not, of course. As world knowledge grows, the stock of a plant's intangible capital stock, Z, depreciates due to obsolescence. This is the significance of the parameter δ_z in equation (6.6). We emphasize that in the absence of any new investment in Z, a plant's output would not change from one date to the next if the plant's h, K, and N do not change.

From the Plant Technology to the Aggregate Production Function

There is an optimal size plant in this economy if and only if the coefficients on physical capital and intangible capital in (6.7) sum to less than one. The sum of θ_k and θ_z is strictly less than one if and only if $\alpha > \theta_k/(1 - \theta_k)$. In what follows, we make this restriction on the values of α and θ_k.

Suppose that at date $t = 0$ there are $L/\overline{N}$ plants in the economy, where L is the measure of households in the economy and $L/\overline{N}$ is large. Moreover, suppose that all plants have the same initial quality. The maximization problem of a plant at date 0 is to choose the length of the workweek, the amount of physical capital to rent, and the amount of investment in intangible capital at each date to maximize the discounted stream of dividends. Formally, the problem is to maximize

$$\sum_{t=0}^{\infty} p_t[Y_t - w_t(h_t)\overline{N} - r_{kt}K_t - X_{zt}]$$

subject to (6.6) and (6.7) and given an initial intangible capital, Z_0.

Because the firm's problem has a unique solution, in equilibrium, plants that start alike stay alike.[22] No exit or entry occurs in equilibrium. In equilibrium, each plant hires $N_t = \overline{N}$ workers, and the date t product of each plant is given by equation (6.7). Equilibrium aggregate output for this economy is thus the measure of plants, $L/\overline{N}$, times the plant's output, Y_t. The aggregate per capita production relation is, thus,

$$y_t = \lambda(1 + \pi)^{-\theta_z} h_t (1 + \gamma)^{(1-\theta_z-\theta_k)t} k_t^{\theta_k} z_t^{\theta_z},$$

where $\lambda \equiv \mu \overline{N}^{\theta_k + \theta_z}$, $k_t = K_t/\overline{N}$, and $z_t = Z_t/\overline{N}$. Variable k_t is interpreted as the per capita aggregate business physical capital stock, and variable z_t is interpreted as the per capita aggregate intangible capital stock. We can always select the units in which output is measured so that $\lambda = 1$. Additionally, if we define $A(\pi) \equiv (1 + \pi)^{-\theta_z}$, we can write the per capita aggregate production relation as

$$y_t = (1 + \gamma)^{(1-\theta_z-\theta_k)t} A(\pi) h_t k_t^{\theta_k} z_t^{\theta_z}.$$

This is the aggregate production function analyzed in chapter 5. This shows how barriers at the plant level determine a country's relative TFP, $A(\pi)$.

The assumption that all plants are initially alike may seem restrictive; in actuality, it is not. A key feature of the investment technology is that the return associated with a given investment is higher the lower is the plant's current quality. Parente (1995) shows that one implication of this type of investment technology is that it is optimal to allocate investments across firms so that the lower support of the distribution of quality across operated plants is as large as possible. Since the highest investment will occur at those plants with the lowest quality levels, it follows that after a finite number of dates, all plants will have identical intangible capital stocks, provided investment is uniformly bounded away from zero.

The Mapping from Barriers to TFP

The preceding analysis shows how differences in policies across countries that constrain the individual production units map into differences in relative TFP. The constraint we considered affected the amount of resources needed to enhance the plant's quality. For this particular barrier, the map from barriers to TFP is $A(\pi) = (1 + \pi)^{-\theta_z}$.

There are other types of policies that constrain individual production units. For example, a similar type of barrier could apply to investment in physical capital. If both of these constraints exist, the map from barriers to TFP is $A(\pi_z, \pi_k) = (1 + \pi_k)^{-\theta_k}(1 + \pi_z)^{\theta_z}$. Another type of constraint could force plants to hire more workers than are necessary to operate them. If instead of $\bar{N}$ workers, $(1 + \pi_N)\bar{N}$ workers are required, then the mapping is

$$A(\pi_z, \pi_k, \pi_N) = (1 + \pi_N)^{-1}(1 + \pi_k)^{-\theta_k}(1 + \pi_z)^{-\theta_z}.$$

The amount of publicly provided infrastructure and the nature of the contracting technology are other examples of policy-related constraints that affect TFP.

How large must these barriers be to account for the large observed international income differences? The answer is that they do not have to be large. To see why, consider the following numerical example. Suppose for the rich country, $\pi = \pi_z = \pi_k = \pi_N = 0$, and suppose for the poor country, $\pi = \pi_z = \pi_k = \pi_N = 0.92$. Policies in the poor country, therefore, result in costs that are less than two times higher than in the rich country. With the assumption that $\pi = \pi_z = \pi_k = \pi_N$, the effect of relative barriers for differences in relative TFP, and the effect of these differences in relative TFP for relative steady-state incomes, depends only on the sum of θ_k and θ_z. For the exercise at hand, we use $\theta_k + \theta_z = 2/3$, which is consistent with the Japanese postwar growth miracle as well as U.S. steady-state observations. With this capital share and these relative barriers, the TFP of the poor country is $1/3$ of the rich country, and its steady-state per capita NIPA GDP is $1/27$ of the rich country. This income difference is approximately the maximum international income difference observed. This establishes the point that barrier differences need not be large to account for the observed differences in international incomes.

7   Evidence of Barriers to Efficiency

In chapter 6, we considered an economy in which the size of a particular type of barrier that constrains the choice of the individual production units determines total factor productivity (TFP). The equilibrium behavior of this economy is identical to that of the neoclassical growth model but with differences in TFP across countries at a point in time. As discussed at the chapter's end, there are a number of other policy-induced constraints that similarly alter the aggregate production function. Precisely how they affect TFP depends on the nature of the constraints.

In this chapter, we present industry data that provide insight into the nature of the constraints at the plant level and how policy gives rise to these constraints. The examination of these data is what leads us to conclude that the most important constraints are on work practices and the use of more productive technologies. This examination also leads us to hypothesize that whether these constraints exist depends upon whether a government protects industry insiders with vested interests tied to the current production process.

The motivation for examining industry-level data is as follows. First, if policy gives rise to differences in TFP at the aggregate level, then policy almost surely gives rise to differences in TFP at the industry level. Second, industry data have the advantage that the reasons for TFP differences are often transparent. In such cases, there is information as to the nature of the machines used in production and the skills needed to operate this equipment.

The Textile Industry

We begin with some evidence from the textile industry. This industry has played a central role in the industrialization of countries, whether it be England at the beginning of the nineteenth century or Mauritius in recent years. For this reason, a large number of detailed studies of this industry exist.

The first of these studies we review is by Clark (1987). He shows that large differences in TFP in cotton textile mills existed across countries in the early 1900s. He reports that in 1910, labor productivity in the New England and Canadian mills was seven times higher than in the Indian mills. He concludes that these productivity differences were due to the number of looms operated per worker, and not to technologies or the education and physical strength of the workers. The reason for most of the difference in the number of looms operated per worker is not the difference in factor prices. In all but the most productive regions, employers wanted their workers to operate more looms. Evidence of this is found in the conflicts between employers and employees over the number of machines employees operated. In India, this conflict was two versus one loom per weaver; in Russia, three versus two; in France and Mexico, four versus three; and in England, six versus four. The key question that Clark (1987) fails to adequately answer is, Why did these conflicts exist?

A study by Wolcott (1994) provides insight into why these conflicts existed as well as what determined the nature of those conflicts, that is, six versus four looms or two versus one. Wolcott (1994) documents differences in the percentage increase in labor productivity in the cotton mills in India and Japan between 1920 and 1938. In this period, Japanese labor productivity increased by more than 120 percent, while Indian productivity increased by only 40 percent. According to Wolcott (1994), these productivity increases were not associated with purchases of more or better equipment. Rather, these increases were achieved by changes in organization that effectively increased the number of machines operated per worker. Productivity changed less in India because work practices changed less there.

According to Wolcott (1994), these differences in productivity increases reflect differences in labor's ability to resist employers' attempts to increase the number of machines each worker operated. By their very nature, textiles are a product whose demand is inelastic. Because of the inelastic demand for textiles, workers associated the loss of jobs with the implementation of these work practices. Indian workers, therefore, restricted such changes. Japanese workers did not. The mechanism by which Indian textile workers attempted to block the introduction of better work practices was strikes. In the interwar period, roughly 1,000 such strikes occurred. Strikes in Japan, in contrast, were rare.

Why were Indian textile workers far more successful than their Japanese counterparts in their attempts to block these changes in work practices? The answer involves the amount of protection the state afforded textile workers. The state protected textile workers in India. Indeed, were it not for this protection, these strikes would not have been successful. The consequence of preventing better work practices is an inefficient industry that cannot withstand competition from producers from other countries. The Indian state never allowed this foreign competition to be a factor. When the inefficient Indian textile industry was threatened by foreign competition, the Indian government reacted by increasing the tariff rate on imported textiles. In contrast, Japanese textile workers received little protection from the state. There was only one major strike in the Japanese textile industry in this period, and it was quickly broken. The Japanese state not only failed to intervene in this strike, but it also allowed mill owners to terminate the service of strikers.

Why did Indian textile workers have the state's protection and thus have the greater ability to prevent changes in work practices from being implemented, while Japanese workers did not? The answer involves the incentives workers in each country had to secure monopoly rights and obtain the state's protection. Wolcott's (1994) thesis is that Indian workers had the greater incentive to prevent changes in work practices from being implemented because textile workers in India were adult males who expected to spend their entire lifetime working in the mills. In Japan, in contrast, workers typically were illiterate girls from the provinces, who generally worked in the mills only a few years before getting married.

Another important example of the state's not being tolerant of resistance to the introduction of better production methods is England at the beginning of the industrial revolution. The resistance by textile workers to the introduction of better technologies occurred in England at this time. These efforts failed for two reasons. First, the state sometimes ruthlessly put down workers' protests.[23] In 1811–1813, for instance, the British government sent out more troops to put down the Luddite riots than were in Wellington's original peninsular army in 1808 (Mokyr 1990, p. 257). More often than not, however, the state took a far less proactive approach to these conflicts. Resistance failed because the state did not adopt laws making it illegal to use these better practices and it did not prohibit competition between regions.

An illustration of where resistance failed on account of this second reason is provided by Randall (1991). He documents several innovations in the English woolen industry, the adoptions of which were delayed for many years on account of workers blocking them. One of the examples he provides is the attempts of shearers to block the introduction of the gig mill at the end of the eighteenth and beginning of the nineteenth centuries. The shearers were the second largest of the adult male trade groups and the best paid. They were responsible for the finishing of fine cloth. Prior to the gig mill, finishing required raising the nap of the cloth with a hand brush and then applying massive shears to create a smooth and even finish.

The gig mill was not a recent innovation. It had been used for nearly two centuries to examine finished cloth for faults and to repair those faults—a process known as burling and perching. In 1793, this proven technology for perching was found to be suitable for the finishing of fine cloth as well. The gig mill, by mechanizing the nap-raising process, dramatically reduced the labor required for finishing woolen cloth. According to Randall (1991), one man and two boys operating one gig mill could accomplish in 12 hours what it took one man to do by hand in 88 to 100 hours. Because the gig mill was an extremely simple machine, this huge savings dwarfed the gig mill's implicit rental price.

With the gig mill's huge labor savings, its use was certain to spell the end of the livelihood of the majority of shearers. Not surprisingly, the shearers resisted the gig mill's application to the finishing of cloth and were successful in delaying its adaptation to finishing cloth for nearly twenty-five years in some regions. At first, they succeeded through a combination of violence, or threats of violence, and an ancient law regarding the use of gig mills for burling purposes written to prevent deceit by over-stretching.[24] The shearers argued that the use of the gig mill for finishing would "wonderfully impair" or "deceit-fully make" the cloth by overstretching, and thus the law prevented the gig mill's application to finishing. Eventually, the state ruled that the law did not apply to the finishing of cloth. Without this protection, the use of the gig mill could not have been stopped. Even in the regions where resistance was fiercest, namely, Gloucestershire and Yorkshire, the gig mill was eventually adopted. Competition from gig mills in other regions that had been converted over from the perching and burling of cloth left shearers in Gloucestershire and Yorkshire with little incentive to continue their resistance and so they finally gave up.

These examples clearly show that when the state does not put up barriers, better production methods are adopted. These examples provide key insights into why England was the first country to enter modern economic growth and become rich. A more recent example from the textile industry in which increases in productivity followed the removal of barriers is provided by Romer (1993), who describes the events that led to the emergence of the garment industry in Mauritius in 1970. Prior to 1970, the garment industry in Mauritius was insignificant. According to Romer (1993), the government of Mauritius in 1970 removed important barriers to production, which included tariffs on imported machinery and materials and prohibitions on ownership and repatriation of profits. The government also gave implicit assurance that factories would be protected from disruptions and that wage increases would be moderate. Shortly after the removal of these barriers, entrepreneurs, primarily from Hong Kong, opened up shops in Mauritius, and the garment industry flourished.

Subsurface Mining in the United States

Another example of big productivity movements that appear to have been the result of changes in the incentives of factor suppliers to resist more efficient work practices is the U.S. subsurface coal mining industry in the 1949–1994 period. This sector had a strong union that could, at least in the early part of the period, dictate work practices and, to a significant extent, wages. The behavior of price, output, and productivity strongly suggests that the large movements in productivity were the result of the coal mining union using this power in a way that was in the interest of its members.

Figure 7.1 plots the real price of coal versus labor productivity and output. One feature of the plot is that the correlation between the real price of coal and productivity is highly negative. Another feature is that the amplitudes of fluctuation of these two variables are large, with output per hour varying by a factor of over 4 and coal's real price by a factor of 3. A final feature of the data is that there is relatively little variation in the output of coal, with the maximum yearly output being only 1.5 times the minimum yearly output. These observations do not fit with standard supply and demand theory.

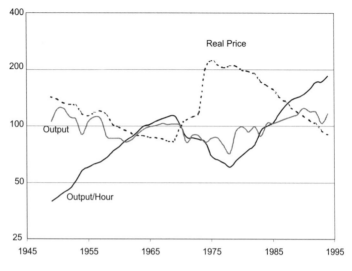

Figure 7.1
U.S. subsurface mining, 1949–1994: Real price, output, and output per hour
Source: U.S. Department of Energy 1996.

Labor productivity increased in the 1949–1969 period by a factor of 3, while the real price of coal fell by 40 percent. The reason for this increase in productivity, particularly in the early part of the period, was the introduction of the boring machine to replace pick-and-shovel technology. The use of boring machines in coal mining was not a technological innovation. These machines were widely used to construct tunnels for many years before their use in coal mining. They had not been used in mining because union contracts had explicitly prohibited their use. They were introduced only when their use benefited the miners. What changed in the late 1940s was that cheap substitutes for coal, namely, oil and natural gas, became available. Cheap oil became available from the Middle East, Venezuela, and the Gulf of Mexico. With the availability of low-priced oil, coal mines that did not increase productivity would be closed. Coal miners, therefore, allowed boring machines to be introduced. There was an explicit agreement that permitted this more efficient mining technology; as part of the agreement, the coal miners subsequently received $20 for every ton of coal mined to finance union pension benefits.

In the 1969–1978 period, labor productivity fell by one-half. This decline in productivity was not the result of new technological knowledge, nor was it the result of marginal mines being operated, as total output did not increase. One reason for the decline was that the price of coal substitutes in the United States increased, and it became apparent that nuclear energy would not be the promised cheap energy source in the foreseeable future. Other reasons for the decline included the breakdown of the cartel of big oil-buying companies and the rise of the cartel of oil-supplying countries. Apparently, union miners lowered productivity to increase the employment of miners. There was a large increase in hours of employment without any increase in output.

The trend in coal productivity reversed itself again in the 1978–1994 period, when productivity increased by a factor of over 3. This increase was not primarily the result of new useable knowledge; at least, we know of no innovation that accounts for this large increase. Our explanation is that, again, miners had no choice but to permit more efficient work practices. If productivity did not increase, the mines would be closed. One factor in increased productivity was a fall in the price of oil. A more important factor, however, was that subsurface coal mines faced increased competition from nonunionized open pit mines in the western United States. There are two reasons for this increased competition. One is that western coal has a lower sulfur content. With the need to reduce sulfur dioxide (the major contributor to acid rain) in the air, the demand for subsurface coal fell. The other reason is that the price of western coal fell with the deregulation of transportation. This further reduced the demand for sub-surface mined coal from the eastern United States. Evidence is strong that productivity increased so much because the reduction in the demand for coal made it in the interest of subsurface coal miners to permit more efficient work practices.

Relative Industry Productivities across Countries

In chapter 4, we reviewed studies by Baily (1993) and Baily and Gersbach (1995) that showed that industry value added per worker varies greatly among the large rich countries. In some industries, the factor is as big as 3. Moreover, no single country is the most productive country in all industries. Productivity in service sector industries is uniformly higher in the United States than in the other large industrialized countries. However, in manufacturing, Japan is more productive than the United States in a number of industries. Here we return to that data to determine whether constraints of the type we have identified elsewhere lie likewise at the heart of these differences.

Baily (1993) and Baily and Gersbach (1995) make the case that these differences in productivity are the direct consequence of constraints that prevent firms from changing current functions and tasks. Those researchers conclude that differences in value added per worker reflect differences in TFP. They rule out differences in physical capital per worker as the reason for these differences after determining that per worker capital stocks differ by very little. They rule out differences in schooling capital or skills per worker as well. Two observations lead to this conclusion. One is that the investigators, after examining the skills of the workers and the skills required for each industry, conclude that workers in each country are qualified to work in their industry in any of the other countries: it is not a matter of the highly productive steelworkers in Japan carrying out sophisticated operations that U.S. and German steelworkers cannot. The other observation, already given in chapter 4, is that if workers in one country are better educated than workers in another, the better educated country should be more productive in all industries in all sectors. This is not the observed pattern. For the same reason, differences in work ethics can be ruled out as a plausible explanation for these differences in value added per worker.

Baily (1993) and Baily and Gersbach (1995) also rule out differences in stocks of useable knowledge in each country. While intellectual propriety rights exist, those rights do not effectively reduce the stock of useable knowledge that a country has at its disposal. As those researchers point out, there are licensing agreements and direct investments that allow proprietary information to be used in different countries. Moreover, there are many multinational corporations operating within the set of large rich countries. Plants of these corporations operated in different countries surely have access to the same knowledge.

What does differ from one country to another, however, is the amount of this knowledge that is used, as well as work practices. Ford Europe, for instance, has failed to adopt Japanese just-in-time production in producing automobiles, but Ford U.S.A. has adopted it. In the beer industry, much of the high technology machinery used in Japanese and U.S. plants is manufactured in Germany.

Yet German breweries fail to use these more productive technologies. The less productive airline sector in Europe vis-à-vis the United States is the result of overstaffing.

Why doesn't Ford Europe use the better technology used by Ford U.S.A.? Why don't German brewers use the equipment German firms sell to the more productive U.S. brewers? And why are European airlines overstaffed? The answer that Baily (1993) and Baily and Gersbach (1995) give to these questions is the same one pointed to by the other studies reviewed in this chapter: namely, constraints that prevent changes in work practices and the use of better technologies. German breweries, for example, cannot adopt the better technologies that are used in the United States and Japan, even though the equipment to run those technologies is made in Germany, because of explicit rules and regulations that govern beer production there. Similarly, zoning laws in the United Kingdom, France, and Germany prevent entry by stores with new retailing formats. European airlines cannot reduce staffing because of union rules and political opposition.

Baily (1993) and Baily and Gersbach (1995) go on to argue that lack of competition explains these differences. Competition as seen in the other case studies reviewed in this chapter is important in understanding differences in productivity across countries at a point in time and within an industry across two points in time. Clearly, constraints that prevent an industry from changing work practices are detrimental to the industry unless the state protects the industry from outside competition. A group of factor suppliers with monopoly rights has no incentive to block the adoption of better production methods if the demand for its services is elastic, which it will be if the group faces competition. We consider the importance of this protection more formally in chapter 8.

8

Monopoly Rights:
A Theory of TFP
Differences

The industry evidence presented in the previous chapter leads us to conclude that the most important constraints are on work practices and the use of more productive technologies. This evidence also leads us to hypothesize that whether or not these constraints exist in an industry depends on whether groups of specialized factor suppliers, namely a group of industry insiders, have monopoly rights tied to current production processes and whether government policies protect these rights.

In keeping with this book's approach, we construct a general equilibrium model to assess the quantitative implications of permitting and protecting monopoly rights for differences in total factor productivity (TFP). We showed in chapter 5 that the difference in steady-state incomes implied by a given difference in TFP depends on capital's share. For capital's share consistent with the Japanese growth miracle, the difference in TFP needed to generate income differences of the magnitude observed in the data is around 3. Therefore, we seek to determine whether protected monopoly rights of groups of factor suppliers to industries can give rise to this factor difference in TFP.

The monopoly rights we consider allow a group in each industry to be the sole supplier of its labor services to all firms using a particular production process. The coalition of industry insiders has the right to dictate work practices and its members' wages for any firm in its industry using this production process. Additionally, the coalition has the right to set its membership size. These monopoly rights are protected via regulation that makes it costly for a group of outsiders to enter the industry with a superior technology. The stronger is this protection, the greater the amount of resources a group of potential adopters of a superior technology must spend to overcome resistance to the use of that superior technology.

The return to entry depends on both the strength of protection and the number of industry insiders. Membership size acts as a deterrent to entry. In each industry, there is a game between the coalition of industry insiders, which has the monopoly right, and a potential entrant. The mechanism by which monopoly rights impede economic progress in our model is, therefore, strategic. When protection is weak, entry occurs since the coalition size that would deter entry would also imply an inadequate compensation to retain and attract members. With stronger protection, entry does not occur, and if protection is not too strong, coalition membership is greater than the number of members needed to produce the equilibrium output. Thus, there can be both an inefficient use of an inferior technology and a failure to adopt the better technology under the monopoly rights arrangement that we consider.

We first describe the basic structure of the economy and then the nature of the game between the industry insiders and the potential entrant under the monopoly rights arrangement. We then determine the implications of the monopoly rights of the type we model for TFPs. This we do by considering an economy with the same structure but in which there are no monopoly rights.

The Economy

In this section, we describe the basic structure of the economy, which consists of a household sector, an industrial sector, and a farm sector. Industrial sector goods can be produced with one of three technologies, each with different labor input requirements per unit of output. In any period, a household is one of three things: a worker in the farm sector, a worker in the industrial sector, or part of a group of entrepreneurs who adopt a technology in the industrial sector.

Household Sector

The household sector contains an atomless measure N of infinitely lived households, each with utility defined over an agricultural good $a(t)$, indexed by date $t \in \{0, 1, 2, \ldots\}$, and differentiated goods $x(i, t)$, indexed by type $i \in [0, 1]$ and by date t. The utility function is

$$\sum_{t=0}^{\infty} \beta^t \left[\left[\int_0^1 x(i, t)^\gamma \, di + \mu a(t)^\gamma \right]^{\theta/\gamma} - 1 \right] \Big/ \theta, \qquad (8.1)$$

where $0 < \beta < 1$, $\gamma < 0$, $\mu > 0$, and $\theta < 1$. This function is strictly concave.

Each household is endowed with one unit of labor services at each date and one unit of land, which provides one unit of land services at each date. Households are not able to sell their land. This assumption is nonbinding and is made to simplify the exposition.

Industrial Sector

In the industrial sector, there are three technologies that can be used to produce each differentiated good. Each of these technologies displays constant returns to scale and has labor services as its only input. Technology $k \in \{0,1,2\}$ for producing the ith industrial good is defined by the constraint

$$X(i,t) \leq \pi_k N(i,t), \tag{8.2}$$

where $N(i,t)$ is the labor input, $X(i,t)$ is the output, and $\pi_0 < \pi_1 < \pi_2$.

No firm-specific investment is required for an individual or group of individuals to adopt any of these three technologies. The reason we abstract from these investments is twofold. First, they are not needed to show that monopoly rights can lead to the nonadoption of the π_2 technology and to the inefficient operation of the π_1 technology. Second, our emphasis in this chapter is on examining whether monopoly rights of the type we consider can give rise to differences in TFP of the order of magnitude suggested by the model in chapter 5, and not on how differences in TFP give rise to differences in capital stocks.

Farm Sector

In the farm sector, there is a constant returns to scale technology for producing the agricultural good, Y_a, which is described by the nested CES production function:

$$Y_a(t) = \left[\psi \left(\int_0^1 X_a(i,t)^\sigma \, di \right)^{\rho/\sigma} + (1-\psi)(N_a(t)^\alpha L_a(t)^{(1-\alpha)})^\rho \right]^{1/\rho},$$
$$\tag{8.3}$$

where $X_a(i, t)$ denotes the input of the ith differentiated good, $N_a(t)$ the input of labor services, and $L_a(t)$ the input of land services. The parameters satisfy $0 < \psi < 1$, $0 < \alpha < 1$, $0 < \rho < 1$, and $\sigma < 0$.

The assumption that $\sigma < 0$ is made to ensure that the farm sector demand for each differentiated commodity is price inelastic. Similarly, our restriction on the preference parameter γ ensures that household demand for each differentiated product is price inelastic. These assumptions are made to simplify the analysis. Specifically, these assumptions imply that whenever monopoly characterizes an industry, the equilibrium price will be the highest price that deters entry. The assumption that $0 < \rho < 1$ is made to ensure that the composite of intermediate goods produced in the industrial sector is a good substitute for the composite labor-land input.

The Monopoly Rights Arrangement

The monopoly rights pertain to the industrial sector. The farm sector is perfectly competitive. We assume that in each industry, there is a coalition of factor suppliers to firms in that industry that use technology π_1. The initial state of a differentiated good industry is the initial number of these industry insiders in that industry. All industries have the same initial state. A coalition of industry insiders has the right to dictate work practices and the wage rate for any firm that uses the π_1 technology and to limit its membership size. Through choice of work practices, the coalition determines the productivity $\pi_x \leq \pi_1$ of any firm that uses the π_1 technology.

A key element of our abstraction is state protection of monopoly rights. How widespread these monopoly rights are in a country depends largely on the behavior of the state. The state must prevent firms in the industry from changing work practices or production methods that would increase productivity and reduce employment. There are a variety of methods the state can use to accomplish this objective. The state can outright prohibit reductions in employment by writing laws to this effect. In India, for example, firms with more than 100 workers must obtain the government's permission to terminate any worker, and firms of all sizes are subject to state certification of changes in the tasks associated with a job. A less direct but equally effective method involves the state sanction of violence and strikes. Another way the state protects the monopoly rights is by requiring large severance payments to laid-off workers. Additionally, in those instances in which a change in work practices requires the use of imported machines, the state can effectively prevent the implementation of these changes by denying the firm import licenses.

The state must protect the industry from entry by new firms that use more productive methods. The state can protect industry from foreign entry by imposing high tariff rates, imposing stringent quotas, and by prohibiting repatriation of profits. The poorest countries in the world are notorious for having the most restrictive trade policies. In Brazil, for instance, the "Lei do Similar Nacional" effectively prevented imports in all industries where there was domestic production through excessive tariffs. Another way the state can protect industry from domestic entry is by requiring licenses to enter and licenses to expand production. In India, these regulations are common. Also in India, regulations require certain firms to award workers with lifetime employment and require firms with more than twenty-five workers to use official labor exchanges to fill any vacancy. The state can and often does discourage entry by firms that use more productive work practices through the subsidization of existing firms.

Recent revisions to the investment codes of several extremely poor countries give evidence that many of these constraints on the behavior of firms are in place. The revisions were made to give assurance to foreign firms that the state will not interfere with the operation of private firms. The Guinean code of 1987—which, according to Marsden and Belot (1987), is similar to Madagascar's revisions and many other sub-Saharan countries' codes— guarantees the right of private-sector firms to import necessary raw materials and equipment and export production, set and implement their own employment policy, determine their customers and input suppliers, repatriate earnings, and be free of unfair competition from parastatal firms. That countries felt compelled to write such codes is evidence that firms were constrained by the state in setting their employment policies and determining their own suppliers. Whether the promises in these codes are credible is another issue.

Still another way the state goes about protecting monopoly rights is by creating state monopolies. The recent privatization of state-owned enterprises reveals the inefficiency of their work practices and the inferior production methods that were used. Despite these sell-offs, inefficient work practices and the use of inferior production methods are likely to continue at some of these facilities as states continue to protect these rights even after the privatization. In Bangladesh, for example, private buyers of the state-owned jute mills were prohibited for one year from laying off any of the workforce they inherited. After one year, a worker could be laid off but not without a large severance payment. According to Lorch (1988), this payment was between three and five months' wages plus an additional month's wages for every year the worker had been with the firm. In Malaysia, the guidelines for privatization prohibited new owners from reducing their workforce for a total of five years. In Central America, these rights are strongly protected as well. According to Cowan (1990), a worker's rights in state-owned enterprises in Panama are so strongly protected that any private buyer can expect to make severance payments equal to two or three times the worker's annual wages.

Industries in our model are competitive and private. However, our theory applies equally to industries that are either public or private monopolies. What is important is that industries are protected from entry by new firms or expansion by existing firms using better production processes. Given the vast number of forms this protection takes, we do not model any specific type of protection. We simply assume that a group that wishes to enter an industry in which a coalition exists and that wishes to use the π_2 technology must make an investment of $N\phi$ units of labor services to overcome resistance associated with the protection of the monopoly rights. The cost to overcoming resistance increases in proportion to an economy's population. This assumption implies that all results are invariant to population size. No such protection exists with respect to the π_0 technology. Any household can use the π_0 technology to produce a differentiated good at any time without having to overcome this resistance. We assume in the model that monopoly rights are protected as long as the coalition exists. A coalition of industry insiders will exist only if there is a surplus to its members.

A free-rider problem is associated with overcoming resistance. Once one group of outsiders makes the needed investment to overcome this resistance in an industry, in subsequent periods, any person or group can use the π_2 technology in that industry and need not make any investment to overcome resistance. In the period in which resistance is overcome, only the outsiders that make the investment can use the π_2 technology. This is to say that the group incurring the cost of overcoming resistance does not gain monopoly rights to the use of the π_2 technology.

This free-rider problem could be eliminated if the government granted monopoly rights to the use of the π_2 technology to a group overcoming the resistance. However, this is highly unlikely to occur because the government must play a key role in protecting the monopoly rights of industry insiders. If the government were to grant monopoly rights to the use of the superior technology to those groups overcoming the resistance, the government would, in effect, be destroying the rents that it was protecting. Moreover, it is highly unlikely that granting these rights would change the transient nature of the rents earned by those overcoming the resistance. Most surely, groups supplying inputs to the better technology would, over time, gain monopoly rights and capture the monopoly rents. Thus, the monopoly rents earned by those who enter with the superior technology would be short lived, just as they are in the model.

Under the monopoly rights arrangement, there are strategic elements, and care must be taken in defining an equilibrium. The key strategic element is the entry-deterrent role of the coalition size. Coalition members are committed to working in the coalition's industry for the current period. For a sufficiently large coalition membership, we will show that it is not in the interest of a potential entrant to invest in overcoming the resistance so that it can use the π_2 technology.

Equilibrium under the Monopoly Rights Arrangement

Having described the nature of the monopoly rights, we proceed to describe the entry game of an industry. Next, we define a symmetric no-entry steady state, and then we develop a set of necessary and sufficient conditions for such a steady state.

The Game

In each industry, the players are the coalition of industry insiders and a potential entrant. These players take as given the demand for the output of their industry and the wage in the competitive farm sector. These elements can be taken as given because the industry is small in the economy, and the industry's behavior has no consequence for these elements.

In the first stage of this game, each member of the coalition noncooperatively decides whether to remain a member and commit to working in the industry for the current period or move to the farm sector. Leaving is voluntary, so stayers and goers must realize equal utility. For simplicity, we rule out side payments. This assumption implies that if there are both stayers and goers, everyone earns the farm sector wage. In the first stage of the game, the coalition also decides whether to admit new members and, if so, how many. The number of coalition members in the ith industry in the period, $N_x(i)$, consists of those inherited from the past less those members who leave plus those who join. In equilibrium, for the coalition to exist, member compensation must be at least as large as the farm sector wage rate, w_a.

The coalition members are a specialized group of factor suppliers because they are committed to working in the industry for the current period. This is the only reason why coalition members are a specialized factor of production in the model. An alternative structure might have this specialization be the result of technology-specific investments made in past periods.

In the second stage of the game, the potential entrant decides whether to overcome the resistance to the use of the π_2 technology. If the potential entrant does not make the investment needed to overcome the resistance, then in the third stage, the coalition picks the productivity $\pi_x(i) \leq \pi_1$ of firms that use the π_1 technology and the wage these firms must pay workers, $w_x(N_x(i))$. If the potential entrant makes the investment required to overcome resistance, then in the third stage, the coalition picks $\pi_x(i)$ and $w_x(N_x(i))$ and the entrant picks price p_e noncooperatively. Conditional on entry, effectively, there is Bertrand price competition where the entrant has a marginal cost w_a/π_2 and no capacity constraint and the coalition has zero marginal cost and the capacity constraint $\pi_1 N_x(i)$.

The nature of the game, subsequent to the coalition's commitment to a size and the potential entrant's commitment to entry, is that the coalition will make it possible for competitive firms to employ the coalition's members to compete with the entrant through a choice of members' productivity $\pi_x(i)$ and wage $w_x(N_x(i))$. This is required for subgame perfection.

In addition to a subgame perfect equilibrium to the game in each industry, equilibrium requires utility maximization, profit maximization in the farm sector, and market clearing. Households and farmers are price takers.

A Set of Conditions for a No-Entry Equilibrium Outcome

In this section, we develop a set of necessary and sufficient conditions for a symmetric equilibrium with no entry and with no changes in the membership sizes of the coalitions. The numeraire for our economy is the agricultural good. We let $p(i)$ denote the price of the ith differentiated good in units of the agricultural good. For a symmetric steady state with no entry, $p(i) = p$ for all i.

The elements that define a no-entry steady state are the vector of prices, (p, w_a, w_x, r), where r is the rental price of a unit of land; the measure of farmworker households, N_a; the measure of industrial worker households, N_x; consumption allocations, (a_h, x_h) for household type $h \in \{a, x\}$; farm sector allocations, (Y_a, X_a, N_a, L_a); and representative industry allocation, (X, N_x), and productivity, π_x.

Farm Sector Equilibrium Conditions

Agricultural firms act competitively, taking prices as given. Since the production technology is subject to constant returns to scale, we aggregate up to a stand-in firm. The maximization problem of the stand-in agricultural firm is

$$\max_{X_a(\cdot), N_a, L_a} \left\{ Y_a - \int_0^1 p(i)X_a(i)\, di - w_a N_a - rL_a \right\}$$

subject to (8.2).

If $p(i) = p$ for all $i \in [0, 1]$, profit maximization implies equal-size purchases of each intermediate good by the farm sector. We use $F(X_a, N_a, L_a)$ to denote farm output when $X_a(i) = X_a$ for all $i \in [0, 1]$; that is,

$$Y_a = F(X_a, N_a, L_a) \equiv [\psi X_a^p + (1 - \psi)(N_a^\alpha L_\alpha^{1-\alpha})^p]^{1/p}. \qquad (8.4)$$

Maximization of profits with respect to X_a, N_a, and L_a yields the following set of three necessary conditions for equilibrium:

$$p = F_X(X_a, N_a, L_a) \tag{8.5}$$

$$w_a = F_N(X_a, N_a, L_a) \tag{8.6}$$

$$r = F_L(X_a, N_a, L_a). \tag{8.7}$$

Household Sector Equilibrium Conditions

We categorize households by their worker type $h \in \{a, x\}$, where a denotes a farmworker household and x denotes an industrial worker household. For a no-entry steady-state equilibrium, these are the only worker types. The distinction of households by worker type is necessary because these groups have different incomes and, therefore, different demand functions. The incomes of workers in either sector consist of their wages, w_h, and land-rental incomes, r.

A household of type h chooses an infinite sequence of differentiated goods and the agricultural good to maximize the discounted stream of utility subject to the intertemporal budget constraint. The necessary no-entry steady-state conditions for utility maximization are

$$p = \frac{x_h^{\gamma-1} a_h^{1-\gamma}}{\mu} \tag{8.8}$$

and

$$a_h + p x_h = w_h + r \tag{8.9}$$

for all $h \in \{a, x\}$. In equations (8.8) and (8.9), we exploit the steady-state condition that $p(i) = p$ and $x_h(i) = x_h$ for all $i \in [0, 1]$. In equation (8.9), we use the no-entry steady-state condition that income of the type h household is the same every period.

Market-Clearing Conditions

The economy has four types of markets: the labor market, the land rental market, the agricultural good market, and the differentiated good market. The market-clearing conditions are

$$\sum_h N_h x_h + X_a = X \tag{8.10}$$

$$\sum_h N_h a_h = Y_a \tag{8.11}$$

$$N_a + N_x = N \tag{8.12}$$

$$L_a = N. \tag{8.13}$$

Game Equilibrium Conditions

For the economy with monopoly rights, the coalition of factor suppliers to firms in the ith industry that use technology π_1 has the right to specify the price of the coalition members' services, dictate work practices, and control membership in the group. Thus, firms in the ith industry that use the π_1 technology produce

$$X(i) = \pi_x(i) n_x(i),$$

where $\pi_x(i) \leq \pi_1$ is the productivity parameter that results from the work practices chosen by the coalition with the monopoly rights and $n_x(i)$ is the number of coalition members employed in the ith industry. There is free entry of such firms.

The objective of each coalition of specialized factor suppliers is to maximize income per member through a choice of work practices $\pi_x(i)$ and the wage rate $w_x(i)$. All coalition members are employed if

$p(i)\pi_x(i) \geq w_x(i).$

This being the case, a necessary condition for maximizing income per member is

$p(i)\pi_x(i) = w_x(i).$

Because coalition members do not value leisure and $\pi_x(i)$ is a choice variable, without loss of generality, we can and will assume that all coalition members are employed. For this reason, $w_x(i)$ is the compensation per coalition member as well as the wage rate, and $N_x(i)$ is the coalition size as well as the coalition employment.

To determine the necessary conditions for a subgame perfect equilibrium outcome with no entry, we use backward induction. Before proceeding, it is necessary to determine total demand for the ith differentiated good, which is the sum of the farm sector and household sector demands. The farm sector's demand for the ith differentiated good is obtained as follows. Set $p(i)$ equal to the derivative of the farm sector's production function with respect to $X_a(i)$, with $X_a(i')$ equal to X_a for all $i' \neq i$. Solve this equation for $X_a(i)$. The solution is the farm sector's demand. A type h household's demand for the ith differentiated good is obtained from the type h household maximization problem given quantities of the other differentiated goods, x_n, and the quantity of the agricultural good, a_h. To obtain total demand for the ith differentiated good, sum demands over all households and the farm sector.

Backward induction proceeds as follows.

Stage 3 At this stage, $N_x(i)$ has been determined and entry either has or has not occurred. When there has not been entry, industry output is

$X(i) = \pi_x(i)N_x(i).$

Because demand for each differentiated good is price inelastic, the coalition of factor suppliers to the ith industry maximizes its total member compensation by setting its work practices and wage rate so that the price of the ith good is the one at which a firm using the π_0 technology breaks even. This price is

$p(i) = w_a/\pi_0.$

In the relevant case in which the coalition's size is sufficiently large to produce the total quantity demanded at this price, income per coalition member, $w_x(N_x(i))$, is

$$w_x(N_x(i)) = \frac{D(w_a/\pi_0)}{N_x(i)} \frac{w_a}{\pi_0},$$

where D denotes total demand for the ith differentiated good. Work practices of the coalition are

$$\pi_x(i) = \frac{D(w_a/\pi_0)}{N_x(i)}.$$

Membership size is sufficiently large to produce the total quantity demanded if $\pi_1 N_x(i) \geq D(w_a/\pi_0)$.

If there has been entry, the entrant has marginal cost w_a/π_2 and no capacity constraint, while the coalition has zero marginal cost up to the capacity constraint, $\pi_1 N_x(i)$. The coalition has zero marginal cost because with its membership size set at the beginning of the period, the coalition's members are stuck in that industry for the period. In the relevant cases in which the output of the entrant is positive, the entrant's choice of price is

$$p(N_x(i)) = \arg\max_{p} \left\{ \left(p - \frac{w_a}{\pi_2} \right) (D(p) - \pi_1 N_x(i)) \right\}.$$

The first term inside the brackets is the difference between price and marginal cost per unit of output. The second term is the sales accruing to the entrant. The entrant's sales are the total quantity demanded at the chosen price less output from firms that employ coalition members. The reason that firms that hire coalition members supply $\pi_1 N_x(i)$ units of the ith good is that given a price of the entrant, the coalition maximizes per member income by choosing $\pi_x(i) = \pi_1$.

Stage 2 At this stage, given the already determined $N_x(i)$, a potential entrant decides whether to enter. Given this membership size, the potential entrant correctly foresees that if it enters, a firm employing coalition members will produce $\pi_1 N_x(i)$ units of output. Consequently, entry is deterred if

$$\max_p \left\{ \left(p - \frac{w_a}{\pi_2} \right) (D(p) - \pi_1 N_x(i)) \right\} \leq w_a N \phi.$$

The entrant's profits are decreasing in $N_x(i)$. Consequently, there is a smallest $N_x(i)$ which deters entry. We use N_x to denote this coalition size.

Stage 1 At this stage, membership size of the coalition is chosen. The coalition members from the preceding period decide whether to remain in the coalition or move to the farm sector. If the wage rate that each coalition member can earn by maintaining membership is greater than the farm wage rate, the coalition will exist in the period. If the size of the preceding period's coalition is the smallest size that deters entry, N_x, and member compensation for this membership size exceeds the farm wage rate, then the coalition maintains its size in the current period and deters entry. However, if member compensation is less than the wage rate in the farm sector for this initial membership size, then the coalition ceases to exist and entry is not deterred.

This analysis of the equilibrium of the game leads to the following set of necessary conditions for a no-entry steady state: From Stage 2, there is the minimal entry-deterrent condition,

$$\max_{p}\left\{\left(p - \frac{w_a}{\pi_2}\right)(D(p) - \pi_1 N_x)\right\} = w_a N\phi. \tag{8.14}$$

From Stage 3, there are the income per coalition member maximizing conditions,

$$p = w_a/\pi_0, \tag{8.15}$$

$$w_x = \frac{D(w_x/\pi_0)}{N_x}\frac{w_a}{\pi_0}, \tag{8.16}$$

$$w_x = \frac{D(w_a/\pi_0)}{N_x}. \tag{8.17}$$

Finally, from Stage 1, there is the entry-deterrent condition,

$$w_x \geq w_a. \tag{8.18}$$

A no-entry steady-state equilibrium must satisfy equations (8.4)–(8.17) as well as condition (8.18).

Important issues are the existence and uniqueness of a no-entry steady-state equilibrium under the monopoly rights arrangement. Our computational procedure finds all such equilibria, thereby resolving the existence and uniqueness questions for the model economy being studied. This is possible because finding an equilibrium reduces to finding a fixed point of a continuous function of a single unknown.[25]

The Free Enterprise Arrangement

Because we are interested in assessing the quantitative implication of permitting and protecting monopoly rights for differences in TFP, it is necessary to consider an economy in which these rights do not exist. We refer to this arrangement as the free enterprise arrangement. Since monopoly rights do not exist in the free enterprise arrangement, any individual or group of individuals can operate any technology.

The set of necessary and sufficient conditions that we use to find the competitive equilibrium is as follows. The set includes the farm sector equilibrium conditions, the household sector equilibrium conditions, and the market-clearing conditions for the monopoly rights equilibrium: that is, equations (8.4)–(8.13). Since the π_2 technologies are the ones operated in the differentiated good industries and workers are indifferent between working in the industrial and the farm sector, conditions for equilibrium in the industrial sector are

$$p = w_x/\pi_2 \tag{8.19}$$

$$X = \pi_2 N_x \tag{8.20}$$

$$w_x = w_a. \tag{8.21}$$

Conditions (8.4)–(8.13) and conditions (8.19)–(8.21) are necessary and sufficient conditions for a competitive equilibrium in the economy.

The Second Welfare Theorem applies to this economy. Consequently, any allocation that maximizes the representative household's utility is an equilibrium allocation. By standard arguments, this maximization problem has a solution. Uniqueness of equilibrium follows from the facts that the solution to the planners' problem is unique and all competitive equilibria solve the planners' problem given that there is a single type.

Quantitative Findings

In this section, we explore how much larger TFP would be if a country eliminated the protected monopoly rights tied to current work practices. We have constructed a parametric class of tractable model economies in which this policy experiment can be carried out. We now select the parameters to be consistent with a number of observations. We then use the resulting model economy to estimate the consequence for TFP of eliminating these monopoly rights.

In restricting our model economy, we must specify the empirical counterparts of the sectors that produce the Y_a and X goods. The defining feature of the Y_a sector in our model is that there are no protected monopoly rights tied to the currently used technology for producing this good. In poor countries, the largest part of this sector's product consists of agricultural goods. However, it also includes a number of services that are produced and consumed in the household sector of poor countries. This production is not part of measured income and product. In rich countries, much of the production of these same services occurs in the market sector and therefore is part of the measured product. Examples of such services include those produced by hair salons, car repair shops, drycleaners, and restaurants. These considerations lead us to include services of this type in the A sector. In the case of the poor country, these services must be imputed. Consequently, the empirical counterpart of value added in sector Y_a for a poor country is larger than the reported value added in the agriculture sector. In a poor country, such as India, the value added in agriculture is about one-third of the total market product. With the addition of imputed home production, the value-added share of the total product of the Y_a sector is surely closer to one-half than one-third in such countries. In rich countries, the Y_a sector is much larger than the agricultural sector as well. Indeed, the share of the final product that originates in sector Y_a is as large, if not larger, in rich countries than it is in poor countries, given the importance of services in rich countries.

We must also specify the empirical counterpart of a period in the model. A model period represents the amount of time before a group overcoming resistance to the use of the π_2 technology faces competition from firms using that technology. If the time before entry by followers is long, the value of the flow of profits for a group that overcomes resistance is large. The empirical counterpart of this profit period is not the time between innovation and entry by imitators in industries in the rich countries, because that involves the application of newly discovered ideas. For poor countries, what is relevant is the time required to adopt proven technologies. For this reason, we see two years as an upper bound for the length of the model period.

Another issue involves the income side. There is no capital in our model economy. This being the case, for the empirical counterpart of the model, we treat depreciation of tractors and other capital goods as intermediate goods. The particular representative economy in this set has the parameter values that are reported in table 8.1. There are twelve parameters, which may seem like a large number. However, the parameters θ and β do not enter into the steady-state calculation, and σ has a minimal effect on the steady state. The values of θ and β are relevant to the analysis of the next section. The value of β is chosen to be

Table 8.1
Parameter values

Preference parameters	Industrial sector technology parameters	Farm sector parameters
$\gamma = -0.11$	$\pi_0 = 1.00$	$\alpha = 0.86$
$\mu = 1.10$	$\pi_1 = 3.00$	$\psi = 0.23$
	$\pi_2 = 9.00$	$\rho = 0.71$
	$\phi = 0.14$	

Source: Parente and Prescott 1999.

consistent with an annual real interest rate equal to 4.5 percent. The absolute values of the industrial sector technology parameters π_0, π_1, and π_2 likewise do not matter for the results. For this reason, the value of π_0 is set to one. Consequently, there are only eight parameters with values that matter.

The values for π_1 and π_2 are selected to be consistent with what we think are reasonable differences between potential productivities of successful technologies. It is not uncommon for the next technological innovation to be between two and three times more productive than the current technology when these technologies are used efficiently. This leads us to select $\pi_1 = 3.0$ and $\pi_2 = 9.0$.

This leaves six parameters. We select these parameters so that the following equilibrium outcomes hold. The fraction of employment in the model's farm sector is 0.60 with monopoly rights and 0.14 in the free enterprise country. Land rental income relative to the sum of land rental and farm labor incomes is 0.14 in both countries. The intermediate goods' share of total farm product is 0.02 in the monopoly rights country and 0.72 in the free enterprise country. Finally, the rents received by workers in the differentiated goods sectors are 60 percent of the farm wage.

Table 8.2
Comparative performances under the alternative arrangements

	Monopoly rights	Free enterprise
Relative GDP (PPP)	1.00	2.72
Final product shares		
Industrial goods	0.47	0.43
Farm goods	0.53	0.57
Income shares		
Land rents	0.07	0.02
Industrial wages	0.48	0.84
Farm wages	0.45	0.14
Value added shares		
Industrial sector	0.48	0.84
Farm sector	0.52	0.16
Relative wages		
w_x/w_a	1.60	1.00
Industrial sector productivity		
π_x	1.60	9.00
Relative prices		
p_x/p_a	0.64	0.15

Source: Parente and Prescott 1999.

This implies that $w_x/w_a = 1.6$ in the monopoly rights country.

Before we can compare TFP for the two policy arrangements, aggregate output must be defined. The definition is an important issue because the price of the industrial good relative to the agricultural good differs between the two economies. In making this comparison, we follow the procedure underlying the construction of the purchasing-power parity gross domestic product (GDP) in the Summers and Heston Penn World Tables. (See Kravis et al. 1982.) Table 8.2 reports the equilibrium outcome for the monopoly rights economy and for the free enterprise economy for a parameterization of the model that roughly matches the observations listed above. The effect on output of eliminating monopoly rights is striking. Comparing per capita output between the two economies, we see that eliminating monopoly rights increases output by a factor of 2.72. Since our Y_a sector includes home production of farm households, which is not part of measured GDP and which is much more important in poor countries, standard national accounting methods would result in a difference exceeding three.

This 2.72 factor increase in output is due solely to an increase in TFP, since there is no increase in the labor input and we abstract from capital accumulation. As found in chapter 5, this is the factor difference in TFP that gives rise to the observed difference in income levels between the richest and poorest countries. As table 8.2 shows, an important reason for the lower TFP in the monopoly rights economy is the inefficiency at which the inferior technology is operated: the coalition of factor suppliers operates the π_1 technology at approximately one-half of the technology's productive potential.

The result that the superior technology is not adopted in the monopoly rights economy and that instead the inferior technology is used inefficiently is robust to alternative values of the preference and technology parameters. Only if π_2/π_1 is huge (greater than 7.0) will the equilibrium outcome be characterized by the π_2 technology being used, and being used efficiently with the monopoly rights arrangement.

Our result is quantitatively reasonable along two dimensions. First, as table 8.2 reports, the price of the industrial good relative to the Y_a good is four times higher in the poor country with the monopoly rights arrangement than in the rich country with the free enterprise arrangement. This is roughly the factor difference in the price of investment to consumption goods across rich and poor countries found in the PWT. Second, the parameterization implies a total cost of overcoming resistance that is 43 percent of industry's annual value added. Given that attempts by textile mill owners in India to implement better work practices resulted in industrywide strikes up to eleven months in duration (Wolcott 1994), the implied cost of overcoming resistance in the model seems well within reason.

Compensatory Schemes

Given the large potential increase in TFP and output associated with eliminating monopoly rights, a relevant question is, Why aren't industry insiders having these rights bought off? We address this question in this section. We consider whether some group can benefit by buying off a coalition with the monopoly rights to the π_1 technology. Clearly, society as a whole can finance the needed payments through small lump-sum taxes on all the households that would benefit from the lower price. However, as a practical matter, such a buyoff is difficult, if not impossible, especially in less developed countries. One reason why it is so difficult is that industry insiders with monopoly rights are more than likely better paid than the average citizen. In a democratic society, explicit transfers to members of a group with above-average income are politically unpopular. This difficulty aside, buyoffs have other problems. One is the time inconsistency problem of government policy. If the promised compensation is spread over a number of years, society has an incentive to default on its promise. Lump-sum payments up front do not avoid this problem. With lump-sum payments and normal preferences, those who receive the compensation will save most of it. But society can then tax this wealth by one mechanism or another. Another problem is that there may be no way to preclude a new group of suppliers to firms that use the π_2 technology from attaining monopoly power and increasing the price, thereby eliminating the benefits to the consumers. For these reasons, we restrict our attention to a buyoff by a small group.

Buyoff by a Subset of the Coalition

Consider the ith industry. We hold output, prices, and coalition membership size of all other industries, $j \neq i$, at their values for the monopoly arrangement equilibrium with no entry. Without loss of generality, we take the potential adopting group to be the coalition itself. Since the group itself is adopting the π_2 technology, there is no cost to overcoming resistance. Further, there is no need to keep more workers in the industry than are needed to meet industry demand. Consequently, some of the coalition members can be released into the farm sector. We emphasize that redundant workers can work in the farm sector in the period of the buyoff since the buyoff occurs before coalition members commit to working in the industry. Finally, group income is shared equally among all members, including those who work in the industry and those who work in the farm sector.

If the coalition were to adopt the π_2 technology, it would choose in the period of adoption the number of production workers, N_s, to maximize coalition-member income:

$$[D^{-1}(\pi_2 N_s)\pi_2 N_s + w_a(N_x - N_s)]/N_x, \tag{8.22}$$

where $D^{-1}(\cdot)$ is the inverse demand for the ith differentiated good. The first term in equation (8.22) is the monopoly revenue. The second term is the income earned by those coalition members who work in the farm sector. This maximization is subject to the constraint that the price not exceed w_a/π_1. Since demand is price inelastic, the maximizing price is the highest one deterring entry, and the optimal number of production workers is that number which is needed to produce the quantity demanded at that price. Because the coalition has given up its rights over the π_1 technology, anyone in the economy can use this technology and hire workers at competitive wages. Consequently, the highest price the coalition can charge for the product without bringing on entry in the period is w_a/π_1, and not w_a/π_0. In future periods, all coalition members earn the farm wage rate, since monopoly power associated with the π_2 technology is assumed to last one period.

The coalition will give up its monopoly rights to the π_1 technology if the discounted stream of utility of its members associated with giving up these rights is greater than the discounted stream of utility associated with maintaining the status quo. The discounted stream of utility depends on agents' desire for smooth consumption as well as the rate at which they discount the future. Consequently, a value of the curvature parameter, θ, and a value of the subjective time discount factor, β, must be specified. For the subjective time discount factor, β, a value of 0.92 is consistent with a real annual rate of interest of 4.5 percent, given a model period length of two years. For the curvature parameter, θ, a value of -1.0 is the value typically used in the real business cycle and finance literature.

For these preference parameter values and the technology parameter values listed in table 8.1, adopting the superior technology is counter to the interest of the coalition.

The higher per member income earned in the first period is not high enough to compensate for the lower wages earned in all subsequent periods. This result holds for all values of θ less than zero (when holding β fixed at 0.92) and all values of β between 1.00 and 0.23 (when holding fixed at -1.0).

Transferable Monopoly Rights

The above finding that it is not in the interest of the coalition with π_1 monopoly rights to adopt the π_2 technology depends on the assumption that the coalition does not receive monopoly rights to the π_2 technology. While we think such rights are typically nontransferable, sometimes they are. One notable example is the U.S. coal mining industry, in which boring machines replaced picks and shovels in the middle of the twentieth century. We therefore consider the following case of transferable monopoly rights.

For this case, the coalition allows any firm to use the π_2 technology as long as that firm hires coalition members, pays wages set by the coalition, and abides by work practices set by the coalition. For the coalition to choose to transfer its monopoly rights, its members must be made better off in terms of expected discounted utility. There are no gains if all members stay in the industry because industry revenue, which goes to the coalition, would fall since the backup technology would be π_1 rather than π_0. Group members no longer employed in the industry therefore move to the farm sector.

Those individuals who lose membership in the coalition will be unemployed and receive a lump-sum payment of τ_ℓ in the current period. In all subsequent periods, they will earn the farm wage. We let N_s denote the number of insiders who stay in the industry and τ_s denote the lump-sum payment per stayer made to finance the payments to the leavers. The wage of a stayer in all periods is

$$w_s = \frac{w_a}{\pi_1} \frac{1}{N_a} D(w_a/\pi_1). \tag{8.23}$$

In equation (8.23), w_a/π_1 is the price that maximizes compensation per worker and $D(\cdot)$ is industry demand. We assume that memberships are terminated by a lottery. In the period of adoption, labor income is $w_s - \tau_s$ for stayers and τ_ℓ for leavers. In future periods, labor income is w_s for stayers and w_a for leavers. The probability of having one's membership continued is N_s/N_x, and the probability of having one's membership terminated is $1 - N_s/N_x$.

A group will transfer its monopoly rights if members' expected utility associated with doing so is greater than the utility of maintaining the status quo. If we let U denote utility as a function of labor income and hold the prices of all other products fixed at their equilibrium value, the condition for the adoption of the π_2 technology is

$$\max_{N_s, \tau_s, \tau_\ell} \left\{ \frac{N_s}{N_x} \left((U(w_s - \tau_s) + \frac{\beta}{1 - \beta} U(w_s) \right) \right.$$

$$\left. + \left(1 - \frac{N_s}{N_x} \right) \left(U(\tau_\ell) + \frac{\beta}{1 - \beta} U(w_a) \right) \right\}$$

$$> \frac{1}{1 - \beta} U(w_x).$$

This maximization is subject to the constraint that within the coalition, transfers sum to 0; that is,

$$N_s \tau_s = (N_x - N_s) \tau_\ell.$$

For the numerical example of the previous section with $\beta = 0.92$ and $\theta = -1.0$, it is not in the interest of the industry insiders to transfer their monopoly rights to the π_2 technology. This result holds for all values of β between 0 and 1 (when holding θ fixed at -1.0) and for all values of θ less than -0.40 (when holding β fixed at 0.92). Enhancing monopoly rights to make them transferable does not result in the adoption of the better technology. For our numerical example, the problem for technology adoption is not that there are too few monopoly rights but that there are too many.

9   Conclusion

We began this volume by asking the question, Why are international income differences so large? The answer we have developed in the course of these chapters attributes most of these differences to country-specific policy that directly or indirectly restricts the set of technologies that the individual production units can use. These differences in constraints translate into differences in total factor productivity (TFP) at the aggregate level. We hypothesized that many of these constraints exist on account of monopoly rights that industry insiders with vested interests tied to current production processes have. With the government's protection, these insiders impose restrictions on work practices and provide strong barriers to the adoption of better technologies.

During the course of these chapters we asked a number of additional, albeit related, questions. Namely, we asked why modern economic growth started first in England before continental Europe, why modern economic growth did not begin in China in the late fourteenth century, why the United States forged ahead of Britain in the late nineteenth century to become the world's most productive nation, and why growth miracles occurred in some countries. We now answer these questions in the context of our theory.

Why England before Continental Europe

Our theory accounts well for the fact that modern economic growth started first in England in the late eighteenth century rather than in continental Europe. England at this time did not protect the monopoly rights of insiders. Ekelund and Tollison (1991) document that the protection of monopoly rights declined in England in the three centuries leading up to the industrial revolution. During the Middle Ages, it was common for the crown to raise revenues by awarding monopoly rights. However, between 1500 and 1750 in England, monopoly rights were awarded less frequently. These authors attribute this trend to a steady shift in power away from the crown and to Parliament. This shift occurred on account of checks the feudal lords put on the crown in the thirteenth century. What emerged were two separate political bodies of similar power that competed for the rents associated with these monopoly rights. According to Ekelund and Tollison (1991), this competition effectively increased the cost of securing monopoly rights, as both the royal courts and the common law courts aligned with Parliament disputed the legality of any rights granted by the other ruling body. As a result of this competition, little regulation was in place in the middle eighteenth century in Britain, and no group could successfully block the adoption of the better technologies that innovators developed.

France, in contrast, had no political competition; the crown had all the power to grant monopoly rights and exercised this power to generate revenues. Corbet, the finance minister under the reign of Louis XIV, perfected this art of revenue generation in the seventeenth century. The economic structure of France, consequently, was dominated by government-sanctioned monopolies that were protected by elaborate regulations.

The situation in Spain at that time was similar to the situation in France. The Spanish crown lacked a serious competitor for power. It granted monopolies and controlled the prices of important products, such as grain. Historians frequently cite the rights granted by the Spanish crown to the Mesta, the coalition of sheep owners, as an important reason why the industrial revolution started much later in Spain. In exchange for tax revenues, the Spanish crown granted the Mesta the right to continue to graze and move its herds along traditional migration routes. To protect this right, the crown prohibited the enclosure of arable land. It is believed that the protection of these rights delayed land enclosure and the productivity increases that the land enclosure system allowed.

Despite the fact that France and Spain had political systems that fostered monopoly rights and impeded economic development relative to England, modern economic growth did eventually occur in France and Spain. As Mokyr (1990) argues, modern economic growth could not be stopped in these countries after it began in England because of the competition between these sovereign states. Governments could not stifle economic progress by protecting monopolies while other states were growing. If they were to, they would surely be invaded and conquered by the richer states. On account of this competition, no individual government could afford to protect monopoly rights as strongly as before.

Why Not Earlier in China[26]

The theory also accounts for the failure of China to enter into modern economic growth in the fifteenth century. By all accounts, China was poised to start modern economic growth at that time. Technologically, China was every bit as advanced in the beginning of the fifteenth century as was western Europe just prior to the start of the industrial revolution in the eighteenth century. In fact, China's development experience from 900 to 1250 parallels in many ways the development experience of England from 1500 to 1750. Per capita iron production increased dramatically, population increased, and the price of iron fell by a factor of 4 relative to the price of grain.

China, of course, failed to experience sustained growth in per capita output until 1950. What happened that delayed China's entry into modern economic growth for over five centuries? The evidence points to the same centralization of power that delayed modern economic growth in continental Europe. Prior to the Mongol conquest of China in 1279, China's central government had four competing groups: the emperor, the civil bureaucracy, the military bureaucracy, and the powerful and independent policy critics. There also was a powerful and independent censorate that effectively policed the bureaucracy, thereby keeping corruption at a relatively low level. None of these groups had the power to dominate policy. As a consequence of competition among these four groups, bureaucracies had a limited ability to protect industry insiders with interests vested in currently used production methods. Regions in China were not autonomous economies that could impose tariffs and other barriers to competition from producers in other regions. As a consequence, groups with the ability to block the use of better technologies chose not to block their use. Our view is that the low level of barriers to technology adoption and its efficient use are why China grew in the 950–1250 period.

Subsequent to this period, the level of barriers increased. Following the expulsion of the Mongols in 1368, the structure of government changed, with a highly centralized government emerging. Shortly after the expulsion, the emperor began to consolidate power, first with the trial and execution of the prime minister and the killing of more than 30,000 civil officials and then with the execution of the general of the army and the purge of 15,000 military officials. The consolidation of power by the emperor was completed with the elimination of the policy critics.

Associated with this centralization was a notable increase in the number of state-operated monopolies as well as an increase in state regulation of the economy during this early Ming period, 1368–1450. The state even attempted to monopolize the measurement of time and the calendar. China, in the first half of the fifteenth century, built huge ships, and its fleets sailed as far as east Africa. The objective was to open trade routes with the Indian subcontinent and other parts of southern Asia. In the middle of the fifteenth century, however, the Chinese government explicitly banned ships with more than two masts, effectively restricting shipping to inland waterways. By doing so, China failed to discover the New World and dominate world trade. Chinese trade with the rest of the world declined dramatically subsequent to banning ships with more than two masts in 1450.

Moreover, the emperor fostered a farm-based society. A consequence of this policy was that textiles were produced on the farm with the spinning of the cotton into yarn and the weaving of the yarn into cloth being done by hand. The technology for producing cotton cloth more efficiently in factories was available but was not used. Apparently, the state protected the farmers with a vested interest in the inefficient hand spinning and weaving from efficient textile factories to maintain a stable farm-based society. Given the importance of the textile industry in the industrial revolution, China's failure to enter into modern economic growth in the 1400–1950 period is no surprise.

Associated with this centralization was also a change in the examination for entry into civil service. Individuals now entered civil service by having knowledge of Confucian classics and literature rather than having good administrative skills. According to Edwards (1999), individuals from merchant families came to make up a substantial portion of the civil bureaucracy as a result of this change in the civil service examination. These civil officials then formed guilds, with membership based on region of origin. Guilds consisted of those officials serving in a region who came from the same region. Later, membership in these guilds was expanded to include merchants who had the same region of origin as the civil servants, so that a commercial-bureaucratic complex formed. The officials in these guilds protected merchant members from competition from indigenous merchants. They set weights and standards and worked with local governments to effectively discourage entrepreneurs from starting up factories.

Once this centralization of power was complete, Chinese rulers were able to extinguish technological progress within the country's borders for six centuries. China was able to do this because it lacked the competition or threat of invasion that was critical to western Europe's development. Without this constant threat, the Chinese government had the incentive to protect the monopoly rights of groups with vested interests tied to currently used technologies. Technological innovation that was rapid from 950 to 1250 stopped, and Chinese living standards stagnated until 1950.

Why the United States and Switzerland Did So Well

Today the United States and Switzerland are the richest industrial nations. The reason that they are the leaders is not an abundance of natural resources. If natural resources were so important for development, countries such as Canada, Australia, and Brazil, with their abundant natural resources, would be richer than the United States and Switzerland. What is relevant and unique about the United States and Switzerland is that both countries have states or canton governments with considerable sovereign power, but not so great as to be able to prohibit movement of goods and people between them.

In the United States, the interstate commerce clause grants the federal government the right to regulate interstate commerce. In the latter half of the nineteenth century and first part of the twentieth century, this clause was interpreted to mean that states could not interfere with interstate commerce. A state had to treat products produced in other states the same as products produced within its borders. Consequently, there was free trade between states, and production coalitions within a state had no choice but to use the best existing technology or to go out of existence.

Later in the twentieth century, the interpretation of the interstate commerce clause was broadened to mean that the federal government could regulate businesses. Associated with this extension, the United States ceased to grow richer relative to the large industrial economies of western Europe. Indeed, the United States lost most of its TFP advantage in the second half of the twentieth century. The reason for this loss is that with federal regulations and national coalitions, it often is in the interest of the coalition of factor suppliers to use its political influence to block the best use of technologies in production.

Switzerland has a government system that is similar to that of the United States, with competition between the states or cantons. Indeed, the Swiss constitution of 1874 is modeled after the U.S. Constitution. With free movement of goods and people between states, there are few benefits

to a group of specialized suppliers to have monopoly
rights. If they exercise these rights, competition from firms
in other states leads to the demise of that industry in that
state.

Why Japan Experienced Its Development Miracle

Our theory accounts for development miracles as well
which, in our theory, occur when policies that prevent
firms from making use of readily available technologies
are removed on a permanent basis. Such changes did
occur in Japan after World War II. Japan, after the jolt of
Commodore Perry's visit in 1853 and the Meiji Restoration, experienced modern economic growth. The Japanese
economy, however, grew only slightly faster than the industrial leader from 1870 to 1940 and closed only a small
part of its income gap with the United States over that
period. Japanese productivity increased from about 20
percent to 25 percent of that of the United States in this
period. Beginning in the 1950s, however, something
changed. Japan experienced a growth miracle with per
capita income increasing from less than 20 percent to
about 75 percent of the U.S. level in a mere twenty years.
This was a period of above-average growth for the United
States, which makes this catch-up all the more remarkable.

Certainly there were a number of important policy
changes during the Meiji Restoration that resulted in
modern economic growth starting in Japan in that era.
However, the effect of these policy changes in terms of
the degree by which monopoly rights tied to current
work practices were eliminated was small relative to the
policy changes that followed World War II. Japan was
occupied after World War II and the primary concern of
the U.S. occupiers was that Japan not again become a

highly centralized and powerful military state. The U.S. occupiers, with some success, broke up Japan's industrial-bureaucratic complex and succeeded in creating competing power centers. A more democratic constitution drawn up by the United States replaced the Prussian-derived constitution of the late nineteenth century Meiji era. More competition among groups in a more democratic system limited the ability of government to protect the vested interest groups tied to current work practices. With these changes, a growth miracle followed.

Development Policy: Competition, Free Trade, and Privatization

The policy prescriptions that follow from our theory are clear. To improve living standards, governments of poor countries must stop protecting monopoly rights of industry insiders with vested interests in the current production processes, as well as stop granting new monopoly rights in the future. If the constraints that prevent firms in the poor countries from using readily available technologies and efficient work practices are eliminated, growth miracles will ensue, and the cross-country differences in income levels will be of the order of magnitude of regional differences within countries.

Governments can stop protecting these monopoly rights by promoting competition. If there is intense competition, industry insiders with the right to block efficient production will never exercise this right, because to do so would spell the end of their industry. Moreover, if there is intense competition, a government is less likely to grant these rights in the future. This is because groups of factor suppliers are also less likely to make investments to try to obtain these rights. If an industry is facing competition, there are no rents, and without these rents, there is little incentive for groups of factor suppliers to organize and lobby the state.

Such a policy prescription is hardly new. The idea that monopoly leads to large inefficiencies and retards economic progress can be traced to the writings of Adam Smith and Alfred Marshall. In spite of empirical support, the classical view that monopoly is a detriment to economic growth and development, and hence, competition should be promoted, received little attention over the last half of the twentieth century. Instead, the Schumpetarian view that monopoly rents are needed to provide incentives for the development of better technologies has dominated. Our view is that countries are not poor because incentives to develop new technologies are lacking. The technologies have been developed in other countries, and it is just a matter of using the technology that is best, given factor prices, and using that technology efficiently.

The current dominance of the Schumpetarian view is due to the lack of a theoretical mechanism by which monopoly rights lead to large inefficiencies. There are, of course, some theoretical mechanisms by which monopoly leads to inefficiencies. One mechanism is the consequence of monopoly power creating a gap between marginal rates of substitution and transformation as modeled by Harberger (1954). Another mechanism is the consequence of capitalized monopoly rents on the accumulation of physical capital as modeled by Laitner (1982). Both mechanisms, however, generate inefficiencies that are at most a few percent of gross domestic product (GDP), a number that is small relative to international income differences.[27] In contrast, the monopoly right we consider can give rise to huge inefficiencies.

To promote competition, poor governments can begin by privatizing industries that are not natural monopolies. To some extent this has started in Latin America. Our chapter 8 model treated the product side of the market as perfectly competitive and private. We could equally well have treated the product market as monopolistic and public in our theory. The results are the same. However, as a practical matter, having the industry monopolized instead of competitive, and public rather than private makes it easier for states to protect the monopoly rights of factor suppliers.

To promote competition, governments should foster free trade. The state needs to ensure that goods and services can move freely between regions inside its country's borders and between countries. International trade, thus, matters for development precisely because it is an important source of competition. Even if the number of domestic firms in an industry is small, the competition from foreign firms, in either domestic or international markets, can be a strong enough force to eliminate the resistance to the adoption of better technologies and the efficient use of technologies. Holmes and Schmitz (1995) have formalized this idea in a general equilibrium dynamic model with lobbying costs.

Ferriera and Rossi (1999) document the dramatic increases in productivity in Brazil that followed trade liberalization in the early 1990s. They document that after declining over the 1980s, both output per worker and TFP increased after the trade liberalizations. For example, they report that output per worker for sixteen industries at the two-digit level declined at an average annual rate of 1.61 percent from 1985 to 1990, but thereafter increased at an average annual rate of roughly 6 percent. Associated with this increase in output per worker and TFP is a significant decline in employment and hours. This is precisely what our theory predicts should have happened.

The effect of increased foreign competition on productivity can be dramatic. Galdon and Schmitz (1998) document the effect of increased foreign competition on productivity in iron ore mining in the 1980s. Increased competition from Brazilian iron ore mines had major consequences for productivity in the U.S. mines, which are located in northern Minnesota. Output per unit of input increased by a factor of 2 as competition made it in the interest of the specialized factor suppliers to permit the doubling of productivity. The reason why miners were so reluctant to accept these more efficient work practices is that they were worried about jobs in the region for their children. Perhaps property rights to jobs, along with dynastic considerations, account for the reluctance of the miners to accept a buyout until there is no option. Most of those losing their jobs associated with the change in work practices were highly skilled machinists who had no problem finding good jobs 250 miles away in the Twin Cities.

Final Comment

To conclude, we think that inevitably insiders will gain the power to dictate work practices. Systems are needed in which it is not in the interest of these insiders to exercise this power to block efficient production. One such system is to have a federal government that prohibits states from interfering with interstate commerce and the free movement of goods and people between states. International trade agreements are another mechanism to achieve this objective. With such arrangements, it is not in the interest

of groups with vested interests tied to current work practices to impose barriers to the use of the best available
technology given factor prices. The gains from such practices are huge, not 1 or 2 percent but 1,000 or 2,000 percent. There is no reason why the whole world should not
be as rich as the leading industrial country.

Notes

1. See Maddison 1991 (p. 10) and Bairoch 1993 (pp. 101–108).

2. The procedure underlying the PWTs is described in Summers and Heston 1988 and 1991. Unless otherwise stated, all references to the PWTs refer to the PWT5.6 from 1991.

3. See Hartwell 1966.

4. These four countries are Guatemala, El Salvador, Nicaragua, and Papua New Guinea. Papua New Guinea was not an independent country until 1975.

5. The set of large non–oil-producing countries that achieved 20 percent of the 1985 U.S. level by 1965 consists of thirty-two countries. Only four of these countries failed to double their per capita incomes by 1988. These countries are Chile, Uruguay, Hungary, and the Soviet Union.

6. For the 5 percent starting level, eighty-seven countries achieved this level by 1965. Due to data limitations, it is not possible to determine the starting years for forty-one of these countries. Of the forty-six countries for which we have starting years, only Chad and Mauritania failed to achieve the 10 percent level by 1988.

7. Mankiw et al. (1992) and Chari et al. (1997) come to this conclusion.

8. See Greenwood et al. 1997.

9. If the period is shorter, unmeasured investment relative to GDP is larger, but this is offset by depreciation being smaller relative to GDP.

10. See Jovanovic 1996 and Bessen 1998.

11. Heckman et al. (1998) come up with a similar number using a similar methodology. Mulligan (1998), using a methodology that focuses on time

use, also comes up with a similar number, though the pattern of investment over the life cycle is different.

12. See Musgrave 1992.

13. For example, see Barro 1991 and Mankiw et al. 1992. Bils and Klenow (1998) present some empirical evidence that expected growth in output leads to investment in human capital, rather than human capital investment leading to growth.

14. Lucas (1988) also has a human capital externality that results in the human capital services provided by an individual being an increasing function of the human capital levels of co-workers.

15. For the Lucas 1988 model, $\sigma = 1$. With $\sigma = 1$, there must be a multiplicative constant in the human capital production function.

16. See Klenow and Rodriguez-Clare 1997.

17. For telecommunications, productivity is measured in terms of the number of calls per worker. For commercial banking, productivity is actually measured in terms of an average of three banking functions per worker.

18. If there were population growth in this economy, then there would be entry. As long as population growth were not too large, at subsequent dates, new firms would be identical to existing firms.

19. Rosen (1974) deals with an equilibrium with a continuum of differentiated products. Mas-Colell (1975) introduces this feature into general equilibrium theory. For a formal general equilibrium analysis with such commodity space, see Hornstein and Prescott 1993.

20. This is clearly a simplifying assumption. The amount of spillover will depend on a variety of factors, including the movement of individuals between profit centers. In an interesting paper, Schmitz (1989) studies an economy in which the speed of spillover depends on the technological closeness of industries.

21. For theories of the growth of world knowledge, see Romer 1990 and Grossman and Helpman 1991.

22. See Parente 1995.

23. Perhaps the reason the English government did not tolerate textile workers' protest was that it was fighting wars with France and needed textiles to clothe its armies.

24. This law was Law 5&6 Edward VI c.22.

25. For the algorithm used to compute the equilibrium, see Parente and Prescott 1999.

26. This material is drawn from Edwards 1999.

27. See Kamerschen 1966, Bergson 1973, and Cowling and Mueller 1978.

References

Auerbach, A. J., and L. J. Kotlikoff. 1987. *Dynamic Fiscal Policy*. Cambridge: Cambridge University Press.

Baily, M. N. 1993. "Competition, Regulation, and Efficiency in Service Industries." *Brookings Papers on Economic Activity*, Microeconomics 2:71–130.

Baily, M. N., and H. Gersbach. 1995. "Efficiency in Manufacturing and the Need for Global Competition." *Brookings Papers on Economic Activity*, Microeconomics: 307–347.

Bairoch, P. 1993. *Economics and World History: Myths and Paradoxes*. New York: Harvester Wheatsheaf.

Barro, R. J. 1991. "Economic Growth in a Cross Section of Countries." *Quarterly Journal of Economics* 106:407–443.

Bergson, A. 1973. "On Monopoly Welfare Losses." *American Economic Review* 63:853–870.

Bessen, J. 1998. "The Adoption Costs of Research Development." Unpublished manuscript, Research on Innovation, Wallingford, PA.

Bils, M. and P. J. Klenow. 1998. "Does Schooling Cause Growth or the Other Way Around?" Unpublished manuscript, University of Chicago.

Canadian Minerals Yearbook. 1998. Ottawa: Energy, Mines, and Resources Canada, Minerals.

Chari, V. V., L. J. Christiano, and P. J. Kehoe. 1994. "Optimal Fiscal Policy in a Business Cycle Model." *Journal of Political Economy* 102:617–652.

Chari, V. V., P. J. Kehoe, and E. R. McGrattan. 1997. "The Poverty of Nations: A Quantitative Exploration." Research Department Staff Report no. 204, Federal Reserve Bank of Minneapolis.

Clark, G. 1987. "Why Isn't the Whole World Developed? Lessons From the Cotton Mills." *Journal of Economic History* 47:141–173.

Cowan, L. G. 1990. *Privatization in the Developing World*. Westport, Conn.: Greenwood Press.

Cowling, K., and D. C. Mueller. 1978. "The Social Costs of Monopoly Power." *Economic Journal* 88:727–748.

DeSoto, H. 1989. *The Other Path: The Invisible Revolution in the Third World*. New York: Harper & Row.

Easterly, W. 1993. "How Much Do Distortions Affect Growth?" *Journal of Monetary Economics* 32:187–212.

Edwards, R. 1999. "China's Economic Development Experience, 900–1900 A.D.: A Growth Theory Perspective." Chapter 2 in *Essays in Economic Development*. Ph.D. dissertation, University of Minnesota.

Ekelund, R. B., and R. E. Tollison. 1991. *Mercantilism as a Rent Seeking Society*. College Station: Texas A&M Press.

Ferreira, P. C., and J. L. Rossi. 1999. "Trade Barriers and Productivity Growth: Cross-Industry Evidence." Unpublished manuscript, Fundacoa Getulia Vargas.

Galdon, J. E., and J. A. Schmitz, Jr. 1998. "Tough Markets and Labor Productivity: World Iron-Ore Markets in the 1980s." Unpublished manuscript, Federal Reserve Bank of Minneapolis.

Gollin, D. 1997. "Getting Income Shares Right: Self Employment, Unincorporated Enterprise, and the Cobb-Douglas Hypothesis." Working Paper, Williams College.

Greenwood, J., Z. Hercowitz, and P. Krusell. 1997. "Macroeconomic Implications of Investment-Specific Technological Change." *American Economic Review* 87:342–362.

Grossman, G. M., and E. Helpman. 1991. *Innovation and Growth in the Global Economy*. Cambridge: MIT Press.

Hall, R. E., and C. I. Jones. 1999. "Why Do Some Countries Produce So Much More Output Per Worker Than Others?" *Quarterly Journal of Economics* 114:83–116.

Harberger, A. C. 1954. "Monopoly and Resource Allocation." *American Economic Review* 44:77–87.

Hartwell, R. 1966. "Markets, Technology and the Structure of Enterprise in the Development of the Eleventh-Century Chinese Iron and Steel Industry." *Journal of Economic History* 26:29–58.

Heckman, J. J., L. Lochner, and C. Taber. 1998. "Explaining Rising Wage Inequality: Explorations With a Dynamic General Equilibrium Model With Heterogeneous Agents." *Review of Economic Dynamics* 1:1–58.

Heston, A., and R. Summers. 1996. "International Price and Quantity Comparisons: Potentials and Pitfalls." *American Economic Review* 86:20–24.

Holmes, T. J., and J. A. Schmitz, Jr. 1995. "Resistance to New Technology and Trade Between Areas." *Federal Reserve Bank of Minneapolis Quarterly Review* 19:(winter) 2–17.

Hornstein, A., and E. C. Prescott. 1993. "The Firm and the Plant in General Equilibrium Theory." In R. Becker, M. Boldrin, R. Jones, and W. Thomson, eds., *General Equilibrium, Growth, and Trade*, vol. 2, *The Legacy of Lionel McKenzie*. San Diego: Academic Press, 393–410.

International Monetary Fund. 1994 and 1998. *International Financial Statistics Yearbook*. Washington, D.C.: International Monetary Fund.

Irwin, D. A., and P. J. Klenow. 1994. "Learning-by-Doing Spillovers in the Semiconductor Industry." *Journal of Political Economy* 102:1200–1227.

Jones, C. I. 1994. "Economic Growth and the Relative Price of Capital." *Journal of Monetary Economics* 34:359–382.

Jorgenson, D. W., and K. Y. Yun. 1984. "Tax Policy and Capital Allocation." Harvard Institute of Economic Research Discussion Paper no. 1107.

Jovanovic, B. 1996. "Learning and Growth." In D. Kreps and K. Wallis, eds., *Advances in Economics*. Cambridge: Cambridge University Press, 318–339.

Kamerschen, D. R. 1966. "Welfare Losses From Monopoly." *Western Economic Journal* 4:221–236.

Klenow, P. J., and A. Rodriguez-Clare. 1997. "Economic Growth: A Review Essay." *Journal of Monetary Economics* 40:597–617.

Kravis, I. B. 1959. "Relative Income Shares in Fact and Theory." *American Economic Review* 49:917–949.

Kravis, I. B., A. Heston, and R. Summers. 1982. *World Product and Income: International Comparisons of Real Gross Product*. Baltimore: Johns Hopkins University Press.

Laitner, J. 1982. "Monopoly and Long-Run Capital Accumulation." *Bell Journal of Economics* 13:143–157.

Lorch, K. 1988. "The Private Transaction and Its Longer-Term Effects: A Case Study of the Textile Industry in Bangladesh." Manuscript, Center for Business and Government, Kennedy School of Government.

Lucas, R. E., Jr. 1988. "On the Mechanics of Economic Development." *Journal of Monetary Economics* 22:3–42.

Lundberg, E. 1961. *Produktivitet Och Rantabilitet*. Stockholm: P.A. Norstedt and Soner.

Maddison, A. 1991. *Dynamic Forces in Capitalist Development: A Long-Run Comparative View*. Oxford University Press.

Maddison, A. 1995. *Monitoring the World Economy: 1820–1992*. Paris: Organization for Economic and Co-operation Development.

Mankiw, N. G., D. Romer, and D. N. Weil. 1992. "A Contribution to the Empirics of Economic Growth." *Quarterly Journal of Economics* 107:407–437.

Marsden, K., and T. Belot. 1987. "Private Enterprise in Africa: Creating a Better Environment." World Bank Discussion Paper no. 17.

Mas-Colell, A. 1975. "A Model of Equilibrium with Differentiated Commodities." *Journal of Mathematical Economics* 2:263–295.

Meltzer, A. H. 1993. "Investment and GDP Are Understated." Unpublished manuscript, Carnegie Mellon University.

Mincer, J. 1994. "Investment in U.S. Education and Training." NBER Working Paper no. 4844.

Mokyr, J. 1990. *The Lever of Riches: Technological Creativity and Economic Progress*. New York: Oxford University Press.

Mulligan, C. B. 1998. "Substitution over Time: Another Look at Life Cycle Labor Supply." NBER Working Paper no. 6585.

Musgrave, J. C. 1992. "Fixed Reproducible Tangible Wealth in the United States, Revised Estimates." *Survey of Current Business* 72:106–137.

Pack, H., and R. Nelson. 1999. "The Asian Miracle and Modern Growth Theory." *Economic Journal* 109:416–436.

Parente, S. L. 1994. "Technology Adoption, Learning by Doing, and Economic Growth." *Journal of Economic Theory* 63:346–369.

Parente, S. L. 1995. "A Model of Technology Adoption and Growth." *Economic Theory* 6:405–420.

Parente, S. L., and E. C. Prescott. 1993. "Changes in the Wealth of Nations." *Federal Reserve Bank of Minneapolis Quarterly Review* 17:(spring) 3–16.

Parente, S. L., and E. C. Prescott. 1994. "Barriers to Technology Adoption and Development." *Journal of Political Economy* 102:298–321.

Parente, S. L., and E. C. Prescott. 1999. "Monopoly Rights: A Barrier to Riches." *American Economic Review* 89:1216–1233.

Pomeranz, K. 1998. "East Asia, Europe, and the Industrial Revolution." Unpublished manuscript, University of California–Irvine.

Prescott, E. C. 1998. "Needed: A Theory of Total Factor Productivity." *International Economic Review* 39:525–552.

Prescott, E. C., and J. Boyd. 1987. "Dynamic Coalitions, Growth, and the Firm." In E. C. Prescott and N. Wallace, eds., *Contractual Arrangements for Intertemporal Trade*. University of Minnesota Press, 146–160.

Randall, A. 1991. *Before the Luddites: Custom, Community, and Machinery in the English Woolen Industry, 1776–1809*. Cambridge: Cambridge University Press.

Rebelo, S. 1991. "Long-Run Policy Analysis and Long-Run Growth." *Journal of Political Economy* 99:500–521.

Restuccia, D., and C. Urrutia. 1996. "Public Policy, Price Distortions, and Investment Rates." Unpublished manuscript, University of Minnesota.

Romer, P. M. 1990. "Endogenous Technological Change." *Journal of Political Economy* 98 part 2:S71–102.

Romer, P. M. 1993. "Two Strategies for Economic Development: Using Ideas and Producing Ideas." In L. H. Summers and S. Shah, eds., *Proceedings of the World Bank Annual Conference on Development Economics 1992*. Washington, D.C.: World Bank, 63–91.

Rosen, S. 1974. "Hedonic Prices and Implicit Markets: Product Differentiation in Pure Competition." *Journal of Political Economy* 82:34–55.

Rosenberg, N. 1982. *Inside the Black Box: Technology and Economics*. Cambridge: Cambridge University Press.

Rosenberg N., and L. E. Birdzell. 1986. *How the West Grew Rich: The Economic Transformation of the Industrial World*. New York: Basic Books.

Schmitz, J. A., Jr. 1989. "Imitation, Entrepreneurship, and Long-Run Growth." *Journal of Political Economy* 97:721–739.

Shoven, J. B., and J. Whalley. 1984. "Applied General-Equilibrium Models of Taxation and International Trade: An Introduction and Survey." *Journal of Economic Literature* 22:1007–1051.

Solow, R. M. 1957. "Technical Change and the Aggregate Production Function." *Review of Economics and Statistics* 39:312–320.

Summers, R. 1973. "International Price Comparisons Based Upon Incomplete Data." *Review of Income and Wealth* 19:1–16.

Summers, R., and A. Heston. 1988. "A New Set of International Comparisons of Real Product and Price Levels: Estimates for 130 Countries, 1950–1985." *Review of Income and Wealth* 34:1–25.

Summers, R., and A. Heston. 1991. The Penn World Table (Mark 5): An Expanded Set of International Comparisons, 1950–1988." *Quarterly Journal of Economics* 106:327–368.

U.S. Department of Energy. 1996. *Annual Energy Review 1995*. Washington, D.C.: Energy Information Administration.

Wolcott, S. 1994. "The Perils of Lifetime Employment Systems: Productivity Advance in the Indian and Japanese Textile Industries, 1920–1938." *Journal of Economic History* 54:307–324.

Young, A. 1995. "The Tyranny of Numbers: Confronting the Statistical Realities of the East Asian Growth Experience." *Quarterly Journal of Economics* 110:641–680.

Index

Letter t denotes a table. Letter n denotes an endnote.